Homemaking Blueprints

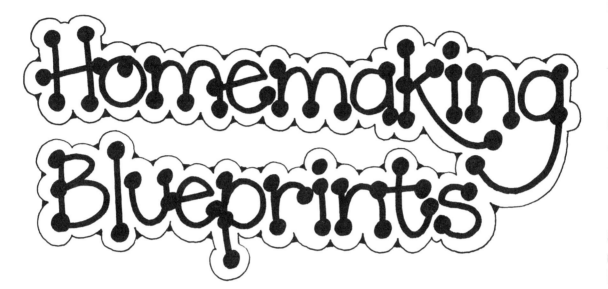

Diane B. Orton
Renee B. Malouf
Illustrated by Annette Ward

Library of Congress Catalog Card Number: 95-79195
ISBN 1-57008-187-5

Fourth Printing, 1997

Printed in the United States of America

Contents

Introduction

Homemaking meetings are an important part of the Relief Society program. According to the *Relief Society Handbook* (1988), "The purposes of the homemaking department are to strengthen individuals and families here and hereafter and to build sisterhood" (p. 6). A successful homemaking meeting can unite the sisters of a ward and help them build stronger and more satisfying family relationships.

Just as building a home requires blueprints, a successful homemaking program requires a well-thought-out plan. A program that attracts the majority of the sisters in the ward and becomes a "no-miss" priority in their lives will make the time spent organizing it worthwhile. Careful planning will make each individual homemaking meeting less work. Make a commitment to plan your homemaking meetings for the next year or, if that is too overwhelming, for six months. Remember, these plans are blueprints and, like house plans, can be changed if necessary.

Begin with the first section of this book. Read the planning techniques and adapt them to fit the individual needs of your ward.

The reward for careful and meticulous planning will be rich blessings for the sisters and families in your ward. Good luck!

Planning an Outstanding Homemaking Program

Organizing a Homemaking Committee

If you are called to be the homemaking counselor or board member, you are given a unique opportunity to help the sisters in your ward become better women, wives, mothers, and homemakers. The first and perhaps most important thing to remember is that you will need help. An effective homemaking program will be one in which you have three to five women who are called to serve as a homemaking committee. Ideally this will be their only calling, but if the size or activity level of your ward makes it impossible to have a specific committee called, perhaps the presidency and teachers in the Relief Society will be willing to serve as your homemaking committee. This committee can help plan the program and then implement those plans.

Sisters who are called to the homemaking committee should understand they have been called to a position that will demand commitment and a considerable amount of time in the beginning planning stages.

Conducting Surveys

Planning a successful homemaking program is much easier when you understand the demographics of the sisters in the ward. Find out what age categories they fall into: young single adults, young mothers, mothers of teenagers, grandmothers, older single adults, and so on. Know whether they serve in the Primary or Young Women organization. Find out how many women work outside the home. Accounting for all of the sisters within the ward boundaries will allow the homemaking committee to plan activities that will appeal to a wide spectrum of sisters.

There is a survey form at the end of this book that you can adapt to fit your needs. The homemaking committee or visiting teachers can help in distributing and collecting the surveys. Be sure to work closely with the Relief Society presidency in this task.

When you distribute the surveys, emphasize the importance of receiving everyone's input. You will get better results if you let the sisters take the survey home and fill it out during a quiet time when they can think about their answers. If the sisters are rushing to fill out the form at homemaking or Relief Society meeting, they will either throw it away or hastily mark the form without giving real thought to their answers.

Make arrangements with the visiting teachers or your homemaking committee to be responsible for getting back all of the surveys. Dividing the responsibility of collecting the surveys will make the task easier.

After the surveys are collected, compile the results and make a copy of them for each member of your homemaking committee. Plan miniclasses centered around the sisters' interests and needs.

An especially important purpose of a survey is to find out about the talents and skills of the sisters in your ward. These skills can then be used as a resource for miniclass teachers at homemaking meeting.

Planning Your Homemaking Meetings

After you have conducted your survey and compiled the results, conduct your first planning meeting. Be enthusiastic and well prepared! It will contribute to the success of the program if the members of the Relief Society presidency come to this first meeting with their support and input.

Copy the planning sheet in the back of this book for the sisters attending the meeting, adapting it as necessary to fit the needs of your ward. Using the survey results, plan classes for at least the next six months.

A variety of classes will attract more sisters to homemaking meeting. It is not always necessary to have four classes as the planning sheet indicates, but unless you have an especially charismatic speaker or important activity, offering a variety of classes will ensure that there is something appealing to everyone.

The round-robin format is another option for classes. Plan four or five classes and divide the sisters into an equal number of groups. The groups rotate from class to class so that each sister has an opportunity to attend every class. The classes should be fifteen to twenty minutes long, depending on the length of your meeting. The miniclass teachers repeat the class until all groups have completed the rotation.

Choosing Miniclass Teachers

Choose teachers for the classes from the sisters in your ward. Some sisters may feel inadequate to teach, but if they have been asked well in advance, and if you offer your help, these sisters will gain the confidence they need.

Just as teaching homemaking classes can be a wonderful tool for building sisters' self-esteem, it can also be a means of reactivating sisters. Contact sisters who may not be active either in Relief Society or in the ward to teach classes. Be careful not to pressure them—remember that love and caring can work miracles!

If you are aware of nonmembers living in your ward boundaries who have special skills, call them to teach a class. You will first need to check with the Relief Society presidency, who will clear it with the bishopric, since circumstances you are not aware of may make it inappropriate to call someone to teach a class.

Don't forget the sisters who serve in the Primary or Young Women organization. Involving these sisters in teaching miniclasses will help them become more involved in the Relief Society homemaking program. Make sure they have plenty of time to prepare for the class.

If absolutely necessary, call sisters outside your ward to teach classes, making sure that sisters called are acceptable to the ward Relief Society presidency and the bishopric.

Always remember that your own ward can be the most important source of teachers. Every sister in the ward has a talent to share with others. If you are enthusiastic and approach them with love and a prayerful heart, most often they will respond to your call. Make sure you are there to help, as requested.

There is a form included in the back of this book that can be used as a guide and organizing tool for class teachers. It may be especially helpful for the inexperienced teacher.

Home Management Lesson Miniclasses

The Relief Society General Board has recommended that a class be held that coordinates with the home management lesson. Since these lessons change from year to year, check the current Relief Society lesson manual for these classes. We have not given suggestions for miniclasses in this area, but a space has been provided on the planning form for such a class. At the end of each lesson there are suggestions for miniclasses that complement that particular lesson.

Holiday Adjustments

If you wish to hold miniclasses that correlate with a particular month's holidays, you will need to check the date of the holiday in relationship to the date of your homemaking meeting. Holidays such as Valentine's Day, St. Patrick's Day, Easter, and Mother's Day come to mind. For instance, if your homemaking meeting comes after Valentine's Day in February and you wish to do a Valentine's craft item, you will need to schedule that craft in January. We have tried to take this fact into consideration when creating our outlines for monthly homemaking meetings, but you will need to adapt the plans to the date of your homemaking meeting. Check the calendar as you plan your classes and be sure you have scheduled a holiday-centered class *before* the holiday.

A Word About Crafts

Counsel has been given not to have too many crafts at homemaking meeting. However, it isn't necessary to totally eliminate them. We feel that shy sisters are more comfortable when they are doing something with their hands. They forget about themselves and think about what they are doing. Additionally, homemaking is a time to get to know one another, and this isn't always possible in a structured, lecture-type class. In a craft activity, sisters who do not know one another will become acquainted while they work.

Crafts can also build traditions within the family. Children remember the seasonal crafts displayed in their home while they are growing up. Crafts geared toward children can also be shared at home and help to build family ties.

Cost is sometimes a real concern. Assess the situations of the sisters in your ward and be sure to offer crafts that are accessible to as many as possible. However, some sisters may have the funds available to spend a bit more and may want to do a more expensive item or project. Your survey results will offer a good indication of what crafts the sisters want and can afford. Try to keep a balance between the cost and quality of the craft item. This balance can be challenging but can be achieved with careful planning.

Book Reviews

We have included book reviews in some of our monthly miniclass plans. Be very cautious when you plan book reviews into your program. Be certain that the books are mainstream books that will not cause controversy in the class.

Working Sisters

One of the most difficult chores is to get working women to attend night homemaking meetings. After working all day they are tired and still have to face the demands of their families. You may want to include a working woman on your homemaking committee. Her input will be invaluable.

Be sure that working sisters complete surveys. Using results from their surveys, plan classes that will help them with their unique needs. Classes on preparing quick and easy meals, streamlining cleaning, and teaching children to help with household chores may appeal to working women. Call a working woman who manages especially well to teach a miniclass and share her insights about how she balances the demands of her job and her family. Remember, you must give her sufficient time to plan the teaching experience into her busy schedule. Giving these sisters an opportunity to teach will also help them feel more a part of the homemaking meeting.

Implementing Your Plan

After you have a plan for the next year or six months, assign the members of the homemaking committee to be in charge of the responsibilities. The form in this book titled "Homemaking Meeting Responsibilities" will help you assign and rotate these assignments.

Don't try to do everything yourself, and don't interfere in assignments you have given. If a homemaking committee member knows you are depending on her and you trust her to do the job, she will respond to your trust. Emphasize at your initial planning meeting that each member of the committee needs to follow through with her monthly assignments. If everyone shares the duties, no one will feel overwhelmed.

Invitations or Announcements

In the monthly miniclass suggestions we have included suggestions for invitations or announcements for homemaking meeting. It is easy to forget a once-a-month homemaking meeting, so a reminder will increase your attendance. While this may seem to be an unnecessary or expensive project, if you will use this idea you will be amazed at how many more women will attend. The invitation reminds them about the meeting, and the effort they see you make in preparing and delivering the reminder will build enthusiasm for the meeting. Adapt the ideas we have given to fit the budget in your ward.

Rotate the responsibility of making the invitations, then deliver them just before the homemaking meeting. Divide your ward into sections, assigning each member of the homemaking committee a delivery section. Dividing this responsibility will make it much less time-consuming.

Try to put the invitation where the sister will be sure to find it. Often this will be on a garage or side door rather than the front door. For maximum impact, check to see which door the family uses most often.

Display Table for Upcoming Months

One of the most effective ways of increasing enthusiasm for your next homemaking meeting is to have a display table for the next month's miniclasses. If you have planned for several months in advance, you can be prepared to set up a table advertising the next month's classes and also get advance sign-up lists for teachers. It is important that you let the miniclass teachers know they must have their class samples ready a month in advance. An attractive display will get the sisters enthused about the next month's meeting.

If you have a class for which it is necessary to limit the number attending, and the sign-up sheet on the display table is filled, you can provide a space on the sign-up sheet for additional sign-ups. Offer the class again if the teacher is willing to teach it more than once. A fun homemaking meeting can be centered around a "Play It Again" theme, with the most-requested classes repeated.

The advance display table can be used during the two weeks before homemaking meeting, allowing sisters to sign up for classes if they missed this chance at the previous meeting. You may also find that sisters who missed homemaking meeting will be disappointed that a class they wish to attend is filled, and they will be at homemaking meeting next month so they can sign up early for a class. Be sure to make this display and sign-up available to the Primary and Young Women organizations. Some wards have set the display up on the kitchen counter next to the Relief Society room two weeks before homemaking meeting. Check with the Relief Society presidency and the bishopric to be sure this is acceptable.

"Share Your Talent" Table

On the Homemaking Meeting Responsibilities form there is space for assigning responsibility for a "Share Your Talent" table. This table should be set up at homemaking meeting and can spotlight a sister in the ward by featuring a special talent she has (such as ceramics or painting), something she collects that would be appealing as a display, or anything else that lets the other sisters in the ward get to know her better. You may not want to do this every month, but it is a good way to positively spotlight a sister and build self-esteem. Be careful, however, that it does not become a source of one-upmanship and intimidation to sisters. You will have to be in tune with the feelings of the sisters to know whether this will work for your ward.

Luncheons

The *Relief Society Handbook* recommends that a light and simple luncheon be held every month. One of the purposes of the luncheon is to help the women in their meal planning at home. Low cost, nutritious meals should be served. In order to encourage the women to use the menus in their homes, place a card at each place setting giving the cost per serving of the meal, and furnish a copy of the recipes used. Encourage the sisters to cook similar meals in their homes.

It often is a challenge to keep the luncheon costs within the bounds of the budget. If cooking classes are held, ask the luncheon committee and the cooking class teacher to coordinate their efforts and use samples from the class for the luncheon.

Work with the luncheon chairman and coordinate the decorations for the luncheon with your monthly theme. Items for these decorations can be borrowed from sisters in the ward rather than spending money from the budget. Many sisters have items in their homes that can be used effectively.

Planning Forms

The forms included in the back of this book are for the most part self-explanatory. You may need to adapt them to your ward's needs, but they provide a basic pattern for planning and implementing your program. Feel free to copy these forms as needed.

A Fun and Useful Idea

One ward helped the sisters remember homemaking meeting by passing out twelve tiny happy-face stickers at homemaking meeting. A note attached to the stickers instructed the sisters to adhere them to their calendar each month so that they would not forget homemaking day. They signed their name as they took their stickers so that the homemaking committee knew who had received the stickers. The committee then made sure that the sisters who were not at homemaking meeting received them.

A Final Word

It certainly would be impossible for one person to carry all of these responsibilities herself, but if you have several people to help you it will be a fun and rewarding experience. The most important point to remember is that careful, advance planning is essential. This will be the most time-consuming part of the program, but if you do this step well, the rest will be easy.

Adapt the planning guides and the monthly homemaking meeting idea section to fit your ward's needs. Prayerfully and lovingly consider the sisters of your ward, and the Lord will bless you for your efforts.

Theme: Rx to Beat the January Blahs: Come to Homemaking Meeting!

Invitation: A form is included which may be copied as needed. If you wish to use a three-dimensional invitation, copy the form and put it in a small zipper-top sandwich bag along with a few small pill-shaped candies. Thread a ribbon or string through the bag to make a loop to hang over the doorknob.

Miniclasses:

Chicken Soup to Soothe the Soul. A chicken soup recipe is included. The class should offer a variety of soup recipes.

Keepsake Birthday Calendar. Keep dates of family birthdays for the year readily accessible by making a simple wall hanging using adhesive webbing. Instructions are included.

Under an Avalanche of Paper? File It or Chuck It! Have a class to motivate the sisters to file the important papers in their homes. Daryl Hoole's book *The Joys of Homemaking,* (Salt Lake City: Deseret Book Co., 1975) has a chapter on filing that could be used as a guide. Don't forget to include a discussion on using the computer to store information.

Beating the Blahs. Have a qualified person teach a class on coping with depression and stress.

Rx to Beat the January Blahs:

Come to Homemaking Meeting!!!

Dr. _____

Cock-a-Noodle Soup

2 whole chicken breasts
1/2 onion, chopped
1 stalk celery, chopped

Cook above ingredients in 5–6 cups of water, adding salt to taste. Remove chicken and cut into bite-size pieces. Strain vegetables from broth and discard, saving broth.

Add the following ingredients to the broth:

1 cup chopped carrots	1 tablespoon lemon juice
1 cup chopped celery	5 cups water
1 cup chopped onion	1/2 teaspoon garlic powder
1/2 teaspoon salt	1/2 teaspoon pepper

Simmer just until vegetables are tender. Add diced chicken to soup along with a good grade of commercial homemade-style egg noodles. Cook until noodles are tender. Garnish with chopped fresh parsley or chopped chives.

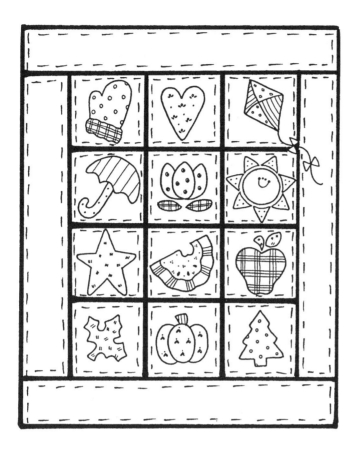 

Keepsake Birthday Calendar

Materials Needed:

2/3 yard (44″–45″ wide) muslin or light-colored fabric for blocks
1/2 yard (44″–45″ wide) fabric for outside borders
1 yard fabric for backing
1 yard cotton batting (Warm & Natural™ is great for wall hangings)
Fabric scraps for monthly designs
HeatnBond® or Wonder-Under® adhesive webbing
Fine-line black marker (Micron Pigma® works well on fabric)
Buttons, embroidery floss, DMC® pearl cotton floss, etc., for embellishing

Instructions:

Cutting: Using muslin, cut twelve 6 1/2″ x 6 1/2″ blocks. Using 1/2 yard fabric, cut two 2 1/4″ x 24 1/2″ strips and two 2 1/4″ x 22″ strips for borders. From backing fabric, cut a 22″ x 28″ piece. Cut a 22″ x 28″ piece of batting.

Wall hanging assembly: All seams are 1/4″. Sew the 12 blocks together, using the diagram shown on the following page. Using the 2 1/4″ x 24 1/2″ strips, add side borders. Using the 2 1/4″ x 22″ strips, add top borders.

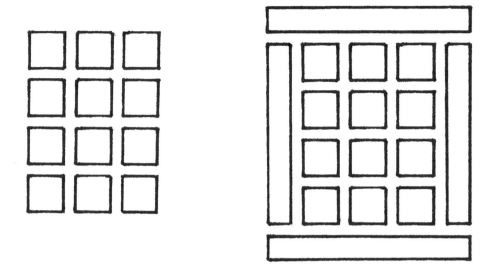

Trace monthly designs (patterns included) on paper side of HeatnBond® or Wonder-Under®. Cut out designs, cutting outside of the lines. Iron designs to the wrong side of your fabric choice, using a dry, warm iron (about 3–4 seconds). Let cool. Cut designs out directly on the lines. Peel off backing paper and place on background monthly blocks, fabric side up. Iron in place.

Using a fine-line marking pen or embroidery floss, add names and dates to remember. Add stitching lines around each block.

Finishing: Place finished top and backing together with batting in the middle. Edges are left raw to give a country look. Using 3 strands of embroidery floss or 1 strand DMC® pearl cotton floss, stitch pieces together around outside edges with a long running stitch. (Note: Start in the middle of hanging, so fabric will not pucker as stitched.)

Hang as desired. If using a hanging rod, use a 3/8" dowel cut to 24" long. Paint with acrylic paints, if desired. You can also hot glue two wood balls with holes drilled in the center to the ends of the dowel.

Hanging tabs: From backing fabric, cut two 2 1/2" x 5" strips. Fold each the long way with right sides together. Sew using 1/4" seams. Turn fabric right side out and press. Tabs will now measure 1" x 5". Fold each tab in half and pin to the background fabric about 2–3" from the top corner, one tab to a corner. Leave 1 1/2" of tab showing above quilt. Stitch in place.

Alternative Themes and Miniclasses

Theme: Happy New Year . . . How to Make It Happen!

Invitation: New Year's party items will be on sale. Purchase noisemakers or other party favors and attach a note telling about homemaking meeting. You could also check with Chinese restaurants or markets and see if they will sell you fortune cookies. Type your message on a slip of paper and tuck it into the fortune cookie.

Miniclasses:

We're Happy When We're Helping. Give ideas for family work charts and how to encourage children to help with family chores.

Stars to Steer By . . . Setting Goals. January is the month for starting anew. Discuss goal-setting techniques.

A Fresh New Start. A diet and exercise class is appropriate for January. You might also have a class on makeup and hair care.

A Place for Everything . . . and Everything in Its Place. Have a class on organizing your home. There are a number of books that could be used as a resource for this miniclass.

Theme: Warm Ideas for Cold Days . . . at Homemaking Meeting

Invitation: Use a cutout of a match or matchbook for your invitation, or cut small patchwork quilt squares and pin on invitation.

Miniclasses:

Hot Potato! Have a cooking class on baked potatoes and toppings.

Keeping Warm with Quilts. Teach how to make a quilt block or have someone do a quilted wall hanging using one of the numerous patterns available.

Warm Up Your Home with Stencils. A how-to class on using stencils in home decorating.

Light Up Your Room with Fireplace Starters. Make cupcake fire-starters. Place cupcake papers in muffin tins. Fill with sawdust to within a half inch of the top. Add 3 tablespoons of melted paraffin wax to each sawdust cake. The wax should seal the surface. Allow to cool, and remove from muffin tin. Light edge of cupcake paper to start fire.

Note: Valentine's Day may come before your next homemaking day. If so, include a Valentine's craft in your January miniclass schedule.

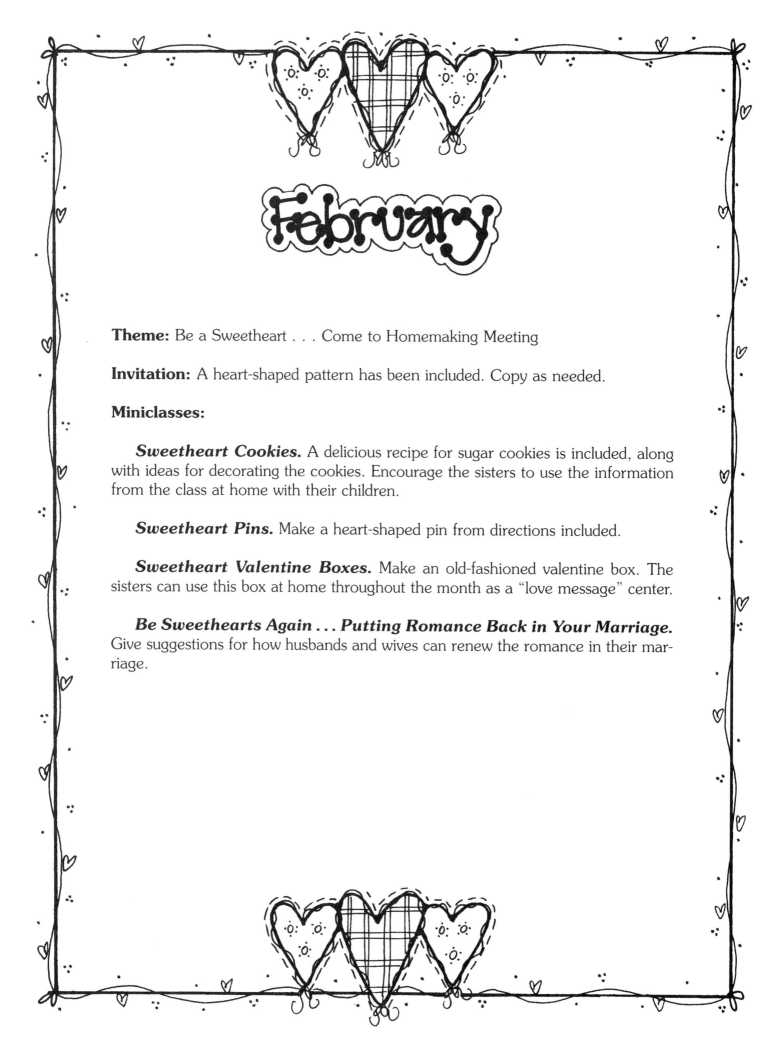

February

Theme: Be a Sweetheart . . . Come to Homemaking Meeting

Invitation: A heart-shaped pattern has been included. Copy as needed.

Miniclasses:

Sweetheart Cookies. A delicious recipe for sugar cookies is included, along with ideas for decorating the cookies. Encourage the sisters to use the information from the class at home with their children.

Sweetheart Pins. Make a heart-shaped pin from directions included.

Sweetheart Valentine Boxes. Make an old-fashioned valentine box. The sisters can use this box at home throughout the month as a "love message" center.

Be Sweethearts Again . . . Putting Romance Back in Your Marriage. Give suggestions for how husbands and wives can renew the romance in their marriage.

Sweetheart Sugar Cookies

1 cup shortening	1 teaspoon grated lemon rind
1 1/2 cups sugar	1 teaspoon grated orange rind
2 eggs, beaten	5 1/4 cups flour
1 teaspoon vanilla	1/2 teaspoon salt
2 tablespoons lemon juice	1 teaspoon baking powder
7 tablespoons orange juice	1 teaspoon baking soda

Combine shortening and sugar, creaming until light and fluffy; stir in eggs, vanilla, juices, and grated lemon and orange rind. Mix well. Combine dry ingredients; add to creamed mixture, mixing well. Put dough into zipper-top bags and refrigerate for several hours or overnight.

To roll: Roll dough to desired thickness on parchment or wax paper which has been cut to size of cookie sheet. Cut shapes and remove edges of dough from between the cookies. Transfer paper to cookie sheet. This method eliminates the hassle of trying to keep the shape of the cookie when you transfer it to the cookie sheet.

Bake at 350 degrees for 10–12 minutes or until edges are just brown. Remove from oven immediately. Don't leave cookies on hot cookie sheet, since they will continue to cook. Remove to cooling racks. When cool, decorate as desired.

Painted Cookies. Make a thin "paint" by combining 1 cup whipping cream with 1/3 cup powdered sugar. Divide the paint among several dishes and add food coloring for desired color. Paint cookies with inexpensive painting brushes.

Fancy Glazed Cookies. Dilute Royal Icing (recipe below) with a few drops of water until the frosting will spread evenly. Spread on cookies and allow to dry until hard. Decorate glazed surface as desired.

Royal Icing. Combine 2 large egg whites (or equivalent amount of meringue powder) and 1/2 teaspoon cream of tartar and beat until frothy. Gradually add 1 package (16 ounces) powdered sugar and beat 5–7 minutes until mixture is stiff (important not to underbeat). Makes about 2 cups. This icing dries quickly. Keep frosting bowl and tips of decorating bags covered with a damp cloth so that frosting will not harden.

Sweetheart Pins

Materials Needed:

Small 1 1/2"–2" wooden heart (available at most craft stores)
Ivory-colored acrylic paint
Assorted buttons (including shirt buttons for rim of heart)
One fancy or heirloom button
Tacky glue
Pin-back (available at craft stores)

Paint wooden heart with acrylic paint and allow to dry. Adhere pin-back to heart with tacky glue. Glue shirt buttons flat around the perimeter of the heart. Glue on remaining buttons, overlapping buttons so that background is not visible. Adhere your heirloom button off-center on the heart. Note: An old watch could be taken apart and the parts of the watch glued among the buttons. Another alternative to buttons might be to use old beads from necklaces or earrings. Tiny charms might also be mixed with the buttons or beads. Use your imagination and make the pin exclusively you! (Thanks to Natalie Carlton of Alpine, Utah, for this idea.)

Sweetheart Valentine Boxes

Beautiful hatboxes can be purchased quite reasonably. Cut a slit in the top of the box so that the love messages or valentines may be slipped into the box without taking off the lid. Any box may be covered with fabric or wrapping paper and decorated with paper doilies and cut-out hearts.

There are a number of excellent craft booklets that give directions for making hatboxes. You could make your own hatbox and decorate as desired.

Family activity. Encourage the sisters to use the valentine boxes as a family activity. The box is displayed throughout the month along with a supply of blank heart-shaped papers. The family members write a "love message" to another family member each day. On family night the messages are distributed.

Alternative Themes and Miniclasses

Theme: Our American Heritage

Invitation: Miniaturize the Constitution. Roll and tie with red, white, and blue ribbon. Attach a slip giving information about homemaking meeting.

Miniclasses:

George's Favorite. A pie-making class should include a favorite cherry pie recipe.

Antiquing with Tea Dyeing. Demonstrate tea dyeing techniques.

Patriotic Cross-Stitch. Teach sisters to cross-stitch on parchment paper, choosing patriotic designs.

The Constitution and the Founding Fathers. A class about the Constitution and the founding of our country is something the sisters could also teach their children on family night. A BYU film titled *A More Perfect Union* is an excellent depiction of this event. At this writing this film is available from KBYU and can be ordered by calling 1–800–298–5298 (credit card order) or mailing a check for $24.95 to KBYU, 2000 Ironton Boulevard, Provo, Utah, 84606. Allow 3–4 weeks for delivery.

Theme: A Celebration of Hearts at Homemaking Meeting

Invitation: Use pattern provided.

Miniclasses:

Heart-Smart Cooking. Give tips for low-fat cooking.

Heart-Shaped Crazy Quilt Doorknob Hanger. Teach the principles of crazy-quilt design.

Heartfelt Greetings. Make your own valentines or heart-shaped gift tags.

Heart-Tugging Poetry. Have a sister who loves poetry share her favorite poetry. The sisters could then teach their children to appreciate good poetry. Note: Check what poetry is being taught—be sure it is appropriate.

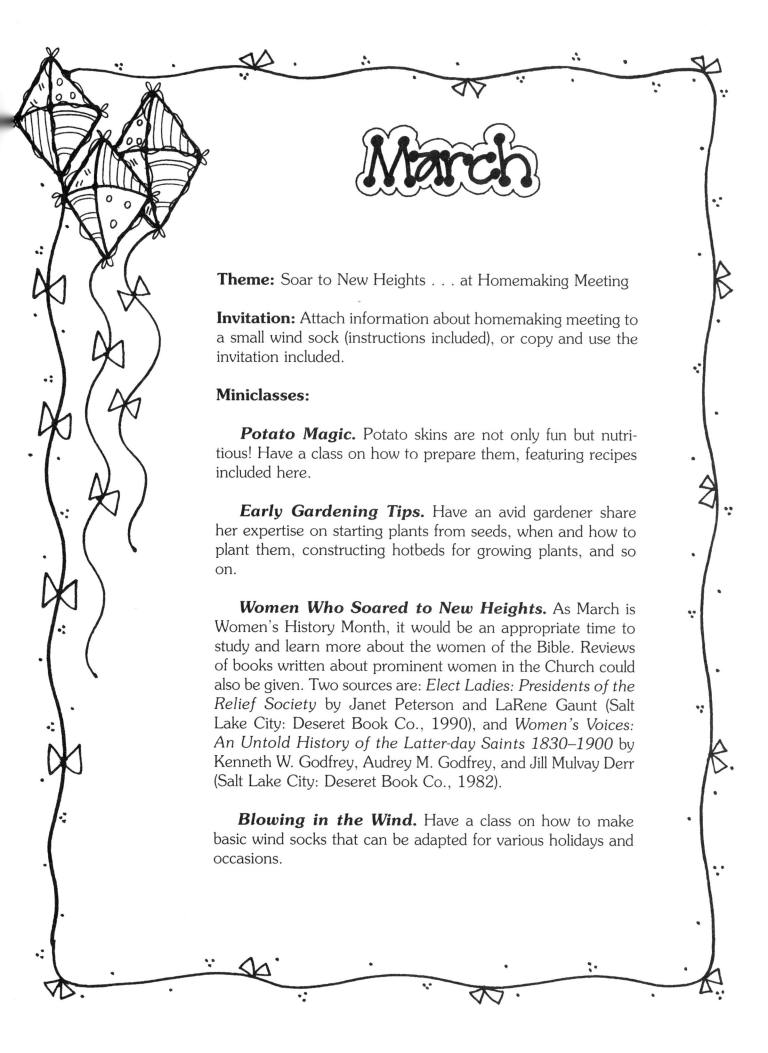

March

Theme: Soar to New Heights . . . at Homemaking Meeting

Invitation: Attach information about homemaking meeting to a small wind sock (instructions included), or copy and use the invitation included.

Miniclasses:

Potato Magic. Potato skins are not only fun but nutritious! Have a class on how to prepare them, featuring recipes included here.

Early Gardening Tips. Have an avid gardener share her expertise on starting plants from seeds, when and how to plant them, constructing hotbeds for growing plants, and so on.

Women Who Soared to New Heights. As March is Women's History Month, it would be an appropriate time to study and learn more about the women of the Bible. Reviews of books written about prominent women in the Church could also be given. Two sources are: *Elect Ladies: Presidents of the Relief Society* by Janet Peterson and LaRene Gaunt (Salt Lake City: Deseret Book Co., 1990), and *Women's Voices: An Untold History of the Latter-day Saints 1830–1900* by Kenneth W. Godfrey, Audrey M. Godfrey, and Jill Mulvay Derr (Salt Lake City: Deseret Book Co., 1982).

Blowing in the Wind. Have a class on how to make basic wind socks that can be adapted for various holidays and occasions.

Instructions for wind sock invitation

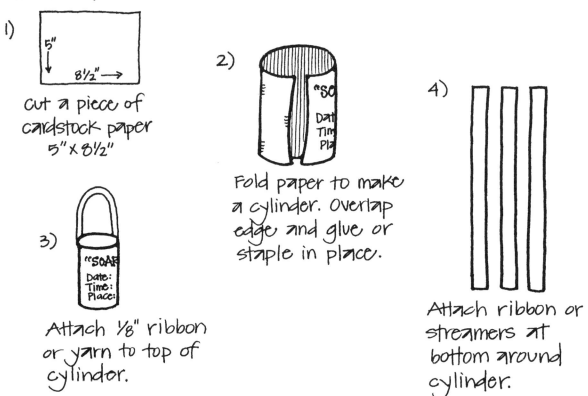

1) Cut a piece of cardstock paper 5" x 8½"

2) Fold paper to make a cylinder. Overlap edge and glue or staple in place.

3) Attach ⅛" ribbon or yarn to top of cylinder.

4) Attach ribbon or streamers at bottom around cylinder.

22

Potato Skins

Russet potatoes are the best to use for making potato skins. Buy a 10-pound bag; it contains more small potatoes and is more economical. The 10-pound bag contains about 27 4-ounce and 10 large potatoes. The 4-ounce potatoes work best for the skins.

Soak the potatoes well to loosen dirt. Scrub with a brush to clean, but be careful not to break the skin. Pierce the skin in several places with a fork to allow steam to escape. Do not wrap in foil, as it will make the skin soft.

Conventional oven. Bake potatoes in a single layer at 400 degrees for 50–55 minutes.

Microwave oven. Arrange potatoes on paper towels, leaving 1"–2" between them. Cook according to oven's directions, turning after half the cooking time. Potatoes will still feel firm when done. Let stand to soften.

When potatoes have cooled enough to handle, slice lengthwise. Scoop out inside, leaving about 1/4" of potato in skin. Refrigerate insides to be used in other recipes. The hollowed-out skins can also be stacked and frozen in plastic bags or refrigerated for up to 4–5 days. If freezing, allow skins to thaw overnight in the refrigerator.

To bake skins. Place skin-side down on a baking sheet. Brush with melted butter; salt and pepper to taste, adding any herbs of your choice. Bake at 425 degrees for 10 minutes or until crispy.

Cheese and Bacon Skins. Bake skins as directed. After removing from oven, add grated sharp cheese and sprinkle with cooked, crumbled bacon bits. Serve with sour cream for dipping.

Crab-Stuffed Skins. To the insides of 6 potatoes, add 1 pound fresh, frozen, or canned crab meat, 1/2 cup butter, 1/2 cup light cream, 1 teaspoon salt, 4 teaspoons grated onion, and 1 cup grated sharp cheese. Fill skins with mixture and top with more cheese and paprika. Bake at 450 degrees for about 15 minutes.

Chili Relleno Skins. Fill skins with diced or whole chili peppers. Top with Monterey Jack cheese and bake at 400 degrees for about 10 minutes.

Tuna Melt Skins. Mix mayonnaise with chunk tuna, season with garlic and onion salt, and place in skins. Top with grated cheese. Avocados may be added between the tuna and cheese layers if desired. Bake at 400 degrees for about 10 minutes, watching closely.

Florentine Skins. Cook 1 package of frozen chopped spinach; drain. Add diced sautéed mushrooms and enough Parmesan cheese to bind. Fill skins and sprinkle with more Parmesan; bake at 400 degrees for about 10 minutes, watching closely.

Mushroom Onion Skins. Sauté sliced mushrooms and onion rings in lots of butter; salt and pepper to taste. Fill skins and top with grated Swiss cheese; bake at 400 degrees for about 10 minutes, watching closely.

Brunch Skins. Scramble eggs with bits of cooked, crumbled bacon; salt and pepper to taste. Fill skins and top with grated Swiss or Gruyère cheese; bake at 400 degrees for about 10 minutes, watching closely.

Broccoli Mornay Skins. Chop and cook fresh broccoli. Place in skins; top with grated cheese. Bake at 400 degrees till cheese melts and then top with toasted bread crumbs and finish baking.

Alternative Themes and Miniclasses

Theme: Reach Your Pot-o'-Gold . . . at Homemaking

Invitation: Make a tiny pot-o'-gold using a miniature Reese's Peanut Butter Cup®. Cut out a tiny rainbow and glue over the cup. Attach to a larger invitation with information about the meeting.

Miniclasses:

Be a Lifesaver. March is Red Cross Month. Check with the Red Cross or your local paramedics about teaching a CPR class. This would be a beneficial class for all sisters.

Chocoholic Mania. March is also National Chocolate Month. What could be more yummy than a class filled with chocolate recipes and ideas?

Houseplant How-To. Have an expert share her knowledge about houseplants and how to care for them.

Holiday Craft. If your homemaking falls before St. Patrick's Day, do a craft for that holiday. If it falls after, do a class featuring an Easter craft.

Theme: Sweet Birthday Wishes . . . at Homemaking

Invitation: Use a birthday cake candle for the invitation. Tie the message on the candle with a brightly colored ribbon.

Miniclasses:

Happy Birthday, Relief Society. Review the book *Elect Ladies: Presidents of the Relief Society* by Janet Peterson and LaRene Gaunt (Salt Lake City: Deseret Book Co., 1990), or discuss Emma Smith and the founding of the Relief Society.

Stamp Frenzy. Use rubber stamps to create gift tags, gift papers, and party invitations.

The Frosting on the Cake. Have a cake decorating class.

Birthday Galas. Have a class on planning children's birthday parties.

April

Theme: Singing in the Rain . . . at Homemaking Meeting

Invitation: Attach your message to a small paper umbrella, or copy and use the umbrella pattern that is included.

Miniclasses:

Refreshing Beverages. Share recipes for punches and beverages to be used for all occasions.

Parasol Topiary. Directions are included for making a paper doily parasol topiary.

Uplifting Music in the Home. Have someone share how to help your family develop an appreciation for good music. Review Jack Christianson's book *Making the Music Decision* (Salt Lake City: Bookcraft, 1995), or have a class on famous composers, on conducting music, or on the hymns and their composers.

Spice Up Your Life . . . with Herbs. Have a class on how to grow and use herbs. Have each sister make and take home a small herb basket.

Superb Slush

1 small package lime gelatin (may also use other flavors)
1 cup sugar
1 quart boiling water
3 lemons
1 large can pineapple juice
3–4 liter bottles of lemon-lime soda

Dissolve gelatin and sugar in boiling water. Add juice of three lemons and pineapple juice. Pour into clean milk cartons or plastic ice cream buckets and freeze. When ready to serve, defrost 45 minutes to 1 hour. Pour into punch bowl and gently stir in soda.

Serves 30.

Parasol Topiary

Materials Needed:

2 6″ white (or colored) round doilies
3/16″ dowel, cut about 8″ long
2″–3″ size clay pot
Glue gun and glue sticks
Dried flowers or sphagnum moss
Floral foam
1/16″ ribbon (optional)
Organdy ribbon (optional)
Acrylic paint (optional)

Using one 6″ doily, fold it into fourths to find center. Unfold. Cutting along one fold line, cut from outer edge to center; glue edges together to form a cone. Using second 6″ doily, fold it into fourths. Unfold. Folding through the middle of each previous fold, fold into eighths. Turn over to other side of doily; fold into sixteenths. You will now have alternate inside and outside folds resembling a parasol.

Glue cone and then folded doily on top of dowel. Dowel may be painted and dried or left natural. You may also wind dowel maypole fashion with 1/16″ ribbon, gluing at top and bottom.

Cut piece of floral foam to fit clay pot, and glue in pot. Carefully place dowel in center of pot, pushing down into foam. Glue around top of foam to hold dowel in place.

Glue dried flowers or moss around base of dowel. Using 1/16″ ribbon or organdy ribbon, tie a bow around dowel or tie a bow and place at base with flowers.

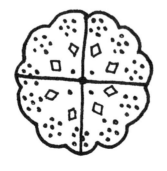 

28

Alternative Themes and Miniclasses

Theme: Look What's Hatching . . . at Homemaking

Invitation: Attach your message to a tiny basket filled with Easter grass and egg candies. Plastic Easter eggs could also be used.

Miniclasses:

Jesus the Christ. What an appropriate time to review James E. Talmage's *Jesus the Christ!* (3rd ed. [Salt Lake City: The Church of Jesus Christ of Latter-day Saints, 1916].)

Panorama Sugar Eggs. Have a class on how to make these fun Easter eggs.

Egg Extravaganza. Share a variety of egg dishes and recipes to use all those leftover hard-boiled Easter eggs.

Creative Easter Baskets. Save money and have fun by learning how to create and assemble your own Easter baskets.

Theme: Grow with Us . . . at Homemaking

Invitation: Attach your message to the back of a seed packet. While stapling the message, attach a ribbon to both sides to make a loop to hang over a doorknob.

Miniclasses:

Let's Stir-Fry. Have someone demonstrate how to stir-fry. Share hints and a variety of recipes.

Spring Clay Pots. Make attractive clay pots by painting with acrylics, sponge painting, or using the new rub-ons that are available.

Bloom Where You Are Planted. Have a presentation on developing a positive attitude and making the most of your life.

Planning Your Victory Garden. Have an experienced gardener share her knowledge about gardening. Send each sister home with plants to start her garden.

Theme: Time to Bloom . . . at Homemaking Meeting

Invitation: Copy and use the invitation included. The invitation has a flower with a clock face that can be used to show the time for your homemaking meeting. A real or silk flower could also be used.

Miniclasses:

Berry Delightful. Have a class on cooking with strawberries while they are in season.

The Scented Bath. Aromatic bath oils in decorative bottles make wonderful gifts. Directions are included for making these now popular items.

Birdhouse Topiary. Birdhouses are all the rage now. Included are directions for making a delightful birdhouse topiary.

Are Things Growing in Your Home? . . . And we don't mean plants! Is it time to do some spring cleaning? Have a class on how to get it clean (and keep it that way!).

Strawberry Cream Cheese Pie

12 ounces cream cheese, softened
2 eggs
3/4 cup sugar
1/2 teaspoon grated lemon peel
1 tablespoon lemon juice
9″ graham cracker pie shell
1 pint fresh strawberries (halved) or 1 package (20 ounces) frozen
    strawberries, slightly thawed
Light corn syrup

Combine cheese, eggs, sugar, lemon peel, and juice; beat until smooth. Pour into graham cracker pie shell and bake 40 minutes at 350 degrees. Cool thoroughly. Chill. At time of serving, arrange strawberries on top of pie and brush with corn syrup.

Graham Cracker Crust

Mix 2 cups graham cracker crumbs with 5 tablespoons melted butter until well blended. Press into a 9″ pie shell.

Grandma's Strawberry Cake

1 box white cake mix
1 box (3 ounces) strawberry gelatin
1 tablespoon flour
1/2 box undrained frozen
   strawberries (about 1/2 cup)

1/2 cup salad oil
4 eggs
1 teaspoon vanilla
1/2 cup water

In large mixing bowl, combine cake mix, gelatin and flour. (Be sure to follow cake mix directions for adding flour for high altitudes.) Add water and oil and mix thoroughly. Add eggs one at a time, beating well after each egg. Add vanilla and frozen strawberries and mix well. Pour into 2 9" pans or a 9" x 13" pan that has been well greased and floured. Bake at 325 degrees for 25–30 minutes. Cool and remove from pans. When completely cooled, frost with Strawberry Frosting.

Strawberry Frosting

Using an electric mixer, mix 1 box (16 ounces) powdered sugar with 1/2 cup butter or margarine. Add 1/2 cup undrained (slightly softened) frozen strawberries and 1 teaspoon vanilla. Blend well.

Strawberry Cake

1 box white cake mix
8 ounces cream cheese, softened
4 cups powdered sugar
Small carton nondairy whipped topping, thawed
1 package strawberry Danish dessert
Fresh strawberries as desired

Mix cake according to the package directions. Cook in 2 9" pans or a 9" x 13" pan. Cool. Mix the cream cheese and powdered sugar together until smooth. Fold in the whipped topping and frost cake. Make the Danish dessert according to package directions. Cool slightly and fold in fresh strawberries. Pour strawberry mixture over the top of the cake. Refrigerate to set.

Alternative Themes and Miniclasses

Theme: Here Comes Summer . . . Get Ready for Summer Fun at Homemaking

Invitation: Use a small hat or a picture of a hat and attach your message.

Miniclasses:

Let's Work Together. Make summer work charts for household chores.

Mini-Vacations. Have a presentation on local vacation spots, points of interest in your area, and inexpensive family activities.

Nibbles and Noshes. Provide ideas and recipes for fun and nutritious summer snacks for your family.

Hats Off to Summer. Decorate straw hats or the popular baseball caps with silk flowers.

Theme: Remembering Our Past . . . Have We Forgotten Memorial Day?

Invitation: Use a flower or a small flag and attach your message.

Miniclasses:

Vintage Bouquets: Preserve the tradition of honoring our dead with flowers by learning how to arrange your own bouquets.

Get Acquainted with Your Ancestors. Have a presentation on how to acquaint your family with their ancestors and how to write family histories.

Down from the Attic. Have a class on restoring those family antiques.

Forgotten Recipes. Have a class featuring old-time recipes. You could also have a class on how to preserve your family recipes.

June

Theme: Everything's Coming Up Roses . . . at Homemaking

Invitation: Cut 5″ circles of net. Place potpourri in center of each circle and fold up. Tie with a ribbon and attach your homemaking message.

Miniclasses:

A round robin format would be appropriate for this month's homemaking meeting. Sisters can rotate from class to class, allowing about 15–20 minutes per class, depending on your time schedule.

Teatime Treats. What to serve for showers and weddings? Learn how to crystallize flowers for decorating cakes and treats, how to make petit fours and delicious beverages, and so on.

Just for Show. A satin or Battenburg lace hanger decorated with ferns and dried flowers makes a lovely bride's gift or Victorian wall accent. (For a round-robin class, this could be just a demonstration.)

Charming Rose Hang-up. This fun tole-painted heart hang-up can be used for a special gift or for yourself. Directions included.

Everlasting Blossoms. Have a class on how to dry and preserve flowers from your summer garden and how to preserve those lovely wedding bouquets.

An Enchanted Garden. Have an expert teach how to grow and care for roses.

Rose Petal Tea Cakes

Make your own tea cakes in a Wilton® individual sponge cake pan following the Wilton® instructions and recipe. You can also purchase the individual sponge cakes (like those used for strawberry shortcake) at most grocery stores.

For frosting:

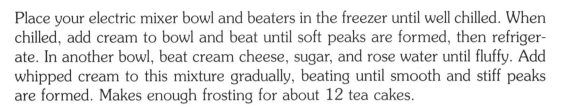

1 cup whipping cream
1 package (8 ounces) cream cheese, softened
1/4 cup powdered sugar
1 tablespoon rose water (optional)

Place your electric mixer bowl and beaters in the freezer until well chilled. When chilled, add cream to bowl and beat until soft peaks are formed, then refrigerate. In another bowl, beat cream cheese, sugar, and rose water until fluffy. Add whipped cream to this mixture gradually, beating until smooth and stiff peaks are formed. Makes enough frosting for about 12 tea cakes.

Frost tops of cakes and decorate with sugared rose petals and leaves. Cover and refrigerate until ready to serve. If using inedible flowers, remove them before eating.

Sugared Flowers

Many flowers can be sugared. Thin-petalled flowers work better than thick-petalled flowers. Edible flowers can also be bought in the produce section of some grocery stores. Some flowers that are edible and work well for sugaring are violets, lilacs, small roses, small lilies, small carnations, and many herb flowers. Try to pick the flowers and blossoms early in the day.

For sugaring you will need:

Granulated sugar (superfine, if available)   Wire whisk
3 egg whites   Wax or parchment paper

Beat egg whites very lightly with a wire whisk. Place sugar in a low bowl or plate. Dip your flower or petals in the egg whites. Place the flower in the sugar and sprinkle sugar on the top to cover petal. Remove the flower or petal carefully from the sugar and place on wax or parchment paper. If doing rose petals, place them on a rolling pin that is covered with wax paper or parchment paper. This will help them retain their rounded shape. Allow flowers to dry at room temperature (drying time will depend on flowers). When flowers have dried, they can be packaged and stored in glass jars. They can then be used to decorate cakes, candies, or petit fours, and are lovely floating in a punch bowl.

Just for Show

Purchase a satin or Battenburg lace hanger. Using hot glue, glue a small piece of sphagnum moss to the center of the hanger. Using dried ferns, flowers, and foliage of your choice, arrange as desired, positioning longer pieces parallel to the hanger arms. (If not using as a wall accent, be sure to leave enough room at ends to hang clothing.) Leave room in the center of the arrangement for a bow and a single large rose or other flower. Using French wire-edge ribbon, make a looped bow in scale to your arrangement and secure to the hanger with floral wire. Glue the bow over the center of the hanger and add center flower. Hanger can be used for hanging bridal dresses, lingerie, and so on, or can just be displayed as a charming wall accent.

Charming Rose Hang-up

Cut a heart shape from about 1/2″ thick wood (can also use any purchased wood hearts). Drill two holes in the top to attach wires for hanging. Paint roses (or any desired flowers) on face of heart with acrylic paints. Allow to dry thoroughly. Put heavy-gauge black wire through the holes, making a hanger, and curl ends of wire. Attach a small torn fabric bow to the top at one side.

Alternate Themes and Miniclasses

Theme: Pop into Summer . . . at Homemaking Meeting

Invitation: Attach your message to a bottle opener, or save soda pop cans and tape your message on a label around the can.

Miniclasses:

A Tisket, a Tasket . . . Make a picnic basket! Be creative and come up with inexpensive ways to make a picnic basket. Half-bushel baskets with elastic covers could be used.

Toteable Goodies. Share recipes for fun and delicious goodies to fill your picnic baskets.

Mom, I'm Bored. Mothers will appreciate ideas for 101—and more—activities to keep their children happy and busy during those summer months!

Summer First Aid. Get prepared for those summer first aid emergencies.

Theme: Friendship Warms the Heart . . . Especially at Homemaking

Invitation: Attach your message to an old-fashioned cut-out paper-doll chain holding hands.

Miniclasses:

A Gift of Love. Have a quilt set up to tie for a service project.

A Charitable Gift. Have a presentation on volunteering at local agencies. Check on projects needed or volunteering at bishop's storehouses or Deseret Industries.

Gifts of Good Taste. Demonstrate how to make treats and goodies that can be shared with neighbors and friends.

Friendshipping Others. This theme is most appropriate for learning how we can better friendship members and nonmembers alike.

This would also be a great time to pick secret sisters for a period of time. The sisters can do it for the month and reveal their identities at the next homemaking meeting.

July

Theme: Have a Star-Spangled Day . . . at Homemaking Meeting

Invitation: Copy the star-shaped invitation that is included. A three-dimensional invitation can be made from a 1/2″ dowel that has been cut into 3″ lengths. Paint the dowels red or blue. Allow to dry and then paint on white stripes and stars to make them look like firecrackers. For a wick, glue a piece of string to the top of the "firecracker."

Miniclasses:

Star-Spangled Salads. Summertime is an excellent time to serve fresh salads.

An Americana Miniquilt. Instructions for a simple miniquilt made with adhesive webbing are included.

Spectacular Family Reunions. Summer is family reunion time. Teach a class on how to have a spectacular family reunion.

Our Country's Heritage. Show the film *A More Perfect Union.* (At this writing it is available from KBYU, 2000 Ironton Boulevard, Provo, Utah, 84606. Call 1–800–298–5298 for credit card orders or mail $24.95 to KBYU. Allow 3–4 weeks for delivery.) The film would be an excellent addition to the ward library.

Heavenly Layered Salad

Salad:

1/2 head iceberg lettuce, chopped
2 tomatoes, chopped
1 large cucumber, thinly sliced
4 large carrots, peeled and thinly sliced
3 stalks celery, thinly sliced
8 green onions, finely chopped
    (chop 2 inches of green stem)
2 cups grated Swiss cheese
1 pound bacon, cooked and crumbled

Dressing:

1 package (8 ounces) cream
    cheese, softened
1 cup mayonnaise
1 cup sour cream
1 teaspoon fresh chopped parsley

Combine all dressing ingredients and mix well. Set aside. Layer vegetables and cheese in a trifle bowl or large glass bowl. Spread the dressing over the layered vegetables, covering completely. Sprinkle with crumbled bacon. Cover and store in refrigerator. About 10 servings.

Spinach Salad I

6 hard-cooked eggs, chopped   1 cup oil
1/2 cup sugar   1/4 cup red wine vinegar
1/2 teaspoon salt   1/2 cup ketchup
2 tablespoons Worcestershire sauce
1 pound bacon, fried and crumbled, saving drippings
1 small onion, chopped, and fried in reserved bacon drip-
    pings until soft

Combine above ingredients. Refrigerate until serving. Serve
over torn spinach greens.

Spinach Salad II

Dressing:

1 1/2 cup oil   1 teaspoon salt
1 pound fresh mushrooms, thinly sliced 1/2 cup sugar
1 cup vinegar   2 tablespoons poppy seeds
1 red onion, cut in half and thinly sliced

Combine above ingredients and marinate overnight or for several hours.

2 packages spinach   1 large head lettuce
1 cup cottage cheese (strain under 1 pound Swiss cheese, grated
    water to remove cream)
1 pound bacon, fried and crumbled

Combine above ingredients in large bowl and toss with marinated onions
and mushrooms. Serve immediately. Serves 10.

Mandarin Orange Salad

1 head lettuce
1 cup celery, chopped
1 can mandarin oranges, drained
1 bunch green onions, chopped (including part of stems)
Sliced almonds, to taste

Combine above ingredients and serve with purchased or
homemade poppy seed dressing.

An Americana Miniquilt

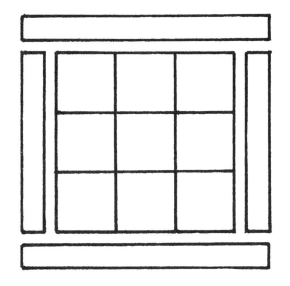 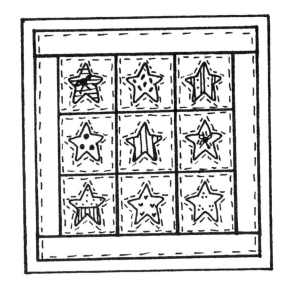

Materials Needed:

15″ x 15″ plain muslin (1/3 yard of 45″ material or 1/2
  yard of 36″ material), cut into nine 4 1/2″ squares
Two 2 1/2″ x 12 1/2″ strips patriotic print (for
  sides of quilt)
Two 2 1/2″ x 16 1/2″ strips complementary patriotic print (for top and bottom of
  quilt—or you may wish to make the sides
  and top and bottom prints all the same)
18 1/4″ x 18 1/4″ complementary patriotic print
  for backing (cut from 1/2 yard of 45″ material)
16″ x 16″ Warm & Natural™ batting or any other
  thin batting
Assorted small patriotic prints for stars
Adhesive webbing for adhering stars
Assorted buttons, ribbons, or charms
Crochet thread or comparable thread for quilting

To sew: Sew the 4 1/2″ squares together with 1/4″ seams in three rows of
three squares. Matching the seams of the squares, sew the three rows together.
  Sew the side pieces (2 1/2″ x 12 1/2″) onto the squares using 1/4″ seams.
  Sew the top and bottom pieces (2 1/2″ x 16 1/2″) onto the top and bottom of
the quilt using 1/4″ seams.

Adhere small pieces of assorted print materials large enough for the star pattern (included here) to adhesive webbing, following instructions that come with the webbing. Be sure you adhere the wrong side of the fabric to the webbing. Trace the star pattern onto the webbing. You will need nine stars. Cut out the stars, pull away the paper, and adhere the stars to the 4 1/2" squares. You might want to use two different fabrics for each or some of the stars, combining fabrics as desired.

To assemble: Lay backing fabric (18 1/4" x 18 1/4") wrong side facing up. Center batting on backing fabric. Lay front of quilt right side facing up over batting, making sure there is an even amount of backing fabric on all edges. To hold layers together, pin or baste each star through all layers, then pin or baste wherever else is needed. Using crochet thread or an equivalent thread, sew a running stitch around the stars about 1/8" from edge of star. Sew a running stitch around each 4" square about 1/4" in from seam lines. Remove basting stitches if used.

To finish: Fold edge of backing over the batting and quilt front. Turn backing under 1/2" and pin. Sew a running stitch around the edge of the backing, thus making a 1" edging around the quilt.

Sew buttons, tiny bows, or charms in the center of the stars.

Alternative Themes and Miniclasses

Theme: Here's the Scoop . . . About Homemaking Meeting

Invitation: Use a cutout of an ice cream cone with 5 scoops of ice cream, each a different color. The name of a miniclass is printed on the ice cream scoops. The date and time of the meeting are printed on the cone.

Miniclasses:

These miniclasses are planned in a round robin format. Each class will be 15–20 minutes long, and the teacher can present the class as many times as necessary to accommodate all of the groups.

Yummy Homemade Ice Cream. Beat the summer heat—make homemade ice cream! A fun family tradition.

Top-It Ice Cream Toppings. Top that homemade ice cream with luscious homemade toppings.

Sizzlin' Summer Barbecues. Abandon that hot kitchen and have a family barbecue.

Patriotic Barbecue Apron. Stencil a simple purchased apron with a patriotic design to wear at your "sizzlin' summer barbecue."

Summer Family Home Evening Ideas. Liven up your family home evening with games, outdoor activities, outings, family olympics, and so on.

Theme: Barefoot in the Park

Invitation: Trace a child's and mother's foot and use the tracings as a pattern. Write a message about homemaking meeting on the feet. Tie the feet together with a ribbon.

Plan a day at a local park for mothers and children. Grandmothers could be encouraged to bring grandchildren if they desire. Play games (water games are especially fun in the summer) and have lunch.

August

Theme: Come and Enjoy a Slice of Summer Fun at Homemaking Meeting

Invitation: A watermelon pattern is included. Copy as needed.

Miniclasses:

   Tantalizing Watermelon Treats. Mouthwatering watermelon treats and fun ways to serve them! Recipes included.

   Preserving Your Produce. Teach the skills necessary to preserve the garden's bounty. A delicious chili sauce recipe is included.

   A Watermelon Welcome. Instructions are included for tole painting a watermelon welcome sign for the front door.

   A Slice of Time. A time management class can help the sisters readjust to the busy school schedule.

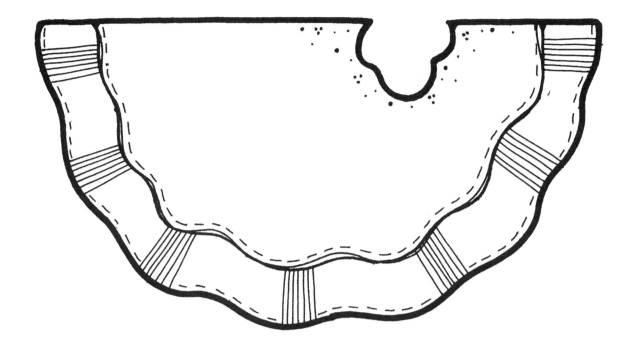

Tantalizing Watermelon Treats

Icy Lollipop Fruits. Cut watermelon and other fruits into round, hexagon, or triangle shapes. Use Popsicle® sticks, barbecue skewers, or sturdy plastic forks to make sticks for your fruit lollipops. A piece of styrene foam (purchased at a craft store or from your local florist) makes a base for your fruit pops. Stick the fruit lollipops securely into foam base and cover the foam with greens from the produce section. To keep lollipops looking fresh and appetizing, spray occasionally with a fine mist of water. Especially effective in a buffet setting!

Ice Cream Watermelon. Chill a watermelon-shaped mold in freezer for 30 minutes. Line chilled mold with a 1″ layer of softened lime sherbet or pistachio ice cream. Cover mold with plastic wrap and freeze until firm, about 3 hours. Cut chocolate chips in half for watermelon seeds. Stir raspberry sherbet or strawberry ice cream to soften slightly and stir in chocolate chip "seeds." Spoon ice cream into center of mold and freeze until firm, about 4 hours. When ready to serve, chill a serving platter for 30 minutes. Unmold ice cream by dipping mold quickly into lukewarm water and inverting onto chilled platter. When serving, cut a slice off the end of the mold to show the inside of the watermelon. A spectacular treat!

Watermelon Dips. These dips can also be used for other fruit.

Maraschino Dip: Stir maraschino cherry juice (to taste) into a 12-ounce jar of marshmallow ice cream topping mixed with an 8-ounce container of non-dairy whipped topping. Stir until smooth.

Strawberry Dip: Defrost frozen strawberries and crush to make about 2/3 cups crushed berries. Stir into a 12-ounce jar of marshmallow ice cream topping until smooth. Add 1/2 teaspoon powdered diet lemonade drink mix into dip (Country Time® is best but can use other brand if desired).

Watermelon Bowls. To display your summer fruits, make a watermelon bowl. For a basket shape, cut top half of watermelon away from both ends, leaving a 1 1/2"–2" section in the middle for a handle. Cut away melon from inside of handle. Scoop melon from inside of watermelon bowl and cut into pieces. Cut a thin slice from bottom of watermelon so that bowl sits straight. Fill with watermelon pieces and other fruit.

To make a scalloped watermelon bowl, cut a thin slice off the bottom so bowl will sit straight. Using a cup or a glass for pattern, trace scallops around top of melon. Carve edge following pattern. Scoop out center. Fill bowl with leftover melon pieces and other fruit.

Preserving Your Produce

Old-Fashioned Chili Sauce

1/2 bushel tomatoes	1 tablespoon cinnamon
9 large onions	1/2 teaspoon cloves
9 large peppers	1 teaspoon allspice
3 1/2 cups sugar	1 tablespoon nutmeg
1 1/2 pints apple cider vinegar	1/2 cup salt
2 tablespoons pepper	

Chop onions and peppers very finely or put through grinder. Peel tomatoes by immersing in boiling water until skins pop open; this only takes about 10 seconds. Remove tomatoes from the hot water with a large spoon and immediately immerse in cold water until cool enough to handle. Slide off skins and cut out stem end of tomato; crush tomatoes. Combine tomatoes, onions, peppers, sugar, vinegar, salt, and spices in large saucepan. Bring to a boil, stirring frequently so it does not burn. Simmer for 5–6 hours over medium-low heat. Continue to stir often so the mixture does not burn. The chili sauce should cook down about one-third. Spoon hot sauce into sterilized bottles; seal tightly. Makes approximately 16–20 half pints.

A Watermelon Welcome

Using illustration as a guide, enlarge to desired size, about 12″ x 9″. Using scroll saw, cut slice from 1/2″–3/4″ pine. Paint as desired with acrylic paints. Attach wire for hanger, curling ends of wire. Tie raffia as illustrated.

Alternative Themes and Miniclasses

Theme: Follow the Yellow Brick Road . . . to Homemaking Meeting

Invitations: Sunflowers are in bloom everywhere in August. Use a real sunflower for your invitation, tying message to stem, or make a sunflower cutout for your invitation.

Miniclasses:

In Its Season. The vegetable garden is at its peak at this time of year. Teach a class on preparing tantalizing vegetable dishes.

Read to Me. Have a local librarian teach a class on children's literature.

Sunflower Topiary. A simple topiary with a sunflower made from bright yellow fabric can be made following the directions given in May for the birdhouse topiary. Tie raffia around the pot.

Don't Get Stranded on the Yellow Brick Road. Change a tire, check the oil . . . you can do it! Keep your automobile in tip-top shape.

Theme: Give It a Whirl . . . at Homemaking Meeting

Invitation: Make pinwheels with paper all-day sucker sticks and construction paper pinwheels. Use a purchased pinwheel for a pattern, reducing size. Attach pinwheel with glass-headed straight pin.

Miniclasses:

Be Prepared . . . Scrumptious Dutch Oven Cooking. Learn to cook in an emergency with Dutch ovens.

Be Prepared . . . Emergency Kits. Make simple kits for each family member.

Be Prepared . . . What Your Family Needs to Know in an Emergency. Be prepared for the emergencies in your area. Have a family emergency plan.

Be Prepared . . . Evaluate Your Food Storage. The Church has published an excellent food storage guide, available at the Church Distribution Center in Salt Lake City.

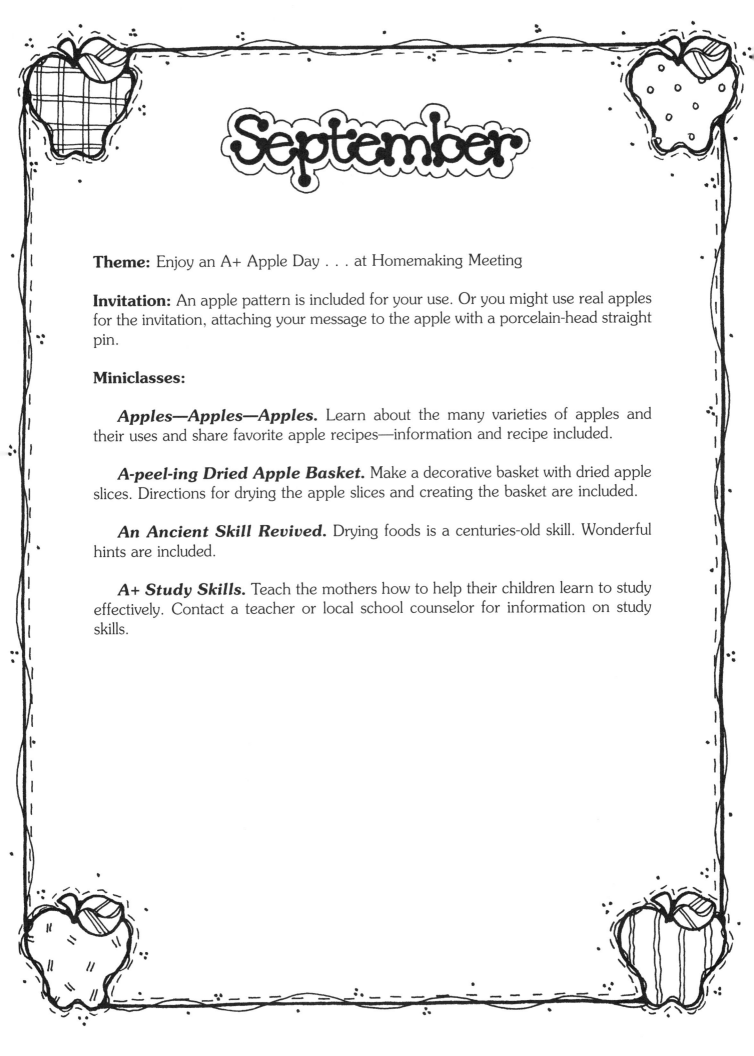

September

Theme: Enjoy an A+ Apple Day . . . at Homemaking Meeting

Invitation: An apple pattern is included for your use. Or you might use real apples for the invitation, attaching your message to the apple with a porcelain-head straight pin.

Miniclasses:

Apples—Apples—Apples. Learn about the many varieties of apples and their uses and share favorite apple recipes—information and recipe included.

A-peel-ing Dried Apple Basket. Make a decorative basket with dried apple slices. Directions for drying the apple slices and creating the basket are included.

An Ancient Skill Revived. Drying foods is a centuries-old skill. Wonderful hints are included.

A+ Study Skills. Teach the mothers how to help their children learn to study effectively. Contact a teacher or local school counselor for information on study skills.

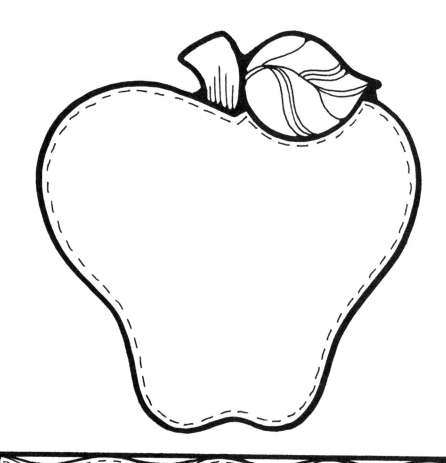

Apple Glaze Bars

Make a favorite pie crust recipe (you will need a crust using approximately 4 cups flour). Divide pie crust into 2 equal balls and roll one onto a jelly roll pan or rectangular cookie sheet. Core, peel, and thickly slice 12 medium apples. Sprinkle apples with a mixture of 2 cups sugar, 2 teaspoons cinnamon, and 1/8 teaspoon nutmeg. Dribble 2 tablespoons lemon juice over apples. Spread apples evenly over pie crust. Roll out second ball of dough and lay over apples. Pinch edges of the two pie crust layers together and prick top to allow steam to escape during baking. Spread top of pie crust with 4 tablespoons softened butter. Bake at 350 degrees for 1 hour. Remove from oven and pour glaze over hot bars.

Glaze: Mix 3 tablespoons lemon juice and 1 1/2 cups powdered sugar until smooth.

Did You Know?

What apple is best for . . .

* *Fruit bowls?* Red Delicious, Winesap, Golden Delicious, Jonathan.
* *General use?* McIntosh, Jonathan, Winesap, Wealthy, Baldwin, Granny Smith.
* *Cooking?* Jonathan, McIntosh, Winesap.
* *Pies?* Gravenstein, Golden Delicious, Winesap, Jonathan, Roman Beauty, Wealthy.

How do I select the best apples?

Firm apples with bright, sparkling color have the best flavor. A rough, reddish-brown skin (russeting) on part of the apple does not affect the quality or flavor of the apple.

How many apples do I buy?

* One pound of apples equals 2 large, 3 medium, or 4–5 small apples and will yield 3 cups peeled, sliced, or diced fruit.
* Two pounds of apples equal 6–8 medium apples and will yield enough slices for one 9″ pie.
* One bushel of apples equals 40 pounds or enough for about 20–24 quarts applesauce or 30–46 quarts apple slices.

How do I store apples?

Store apples in an insulated box in the garage if the days and nights are cool. To insulate a box, place a smaller box inside a larger box and fill the space between the boxes with newspapers, a rug, or a blanket. Apples can also be stored in a straw-lined pit or sunken barrel. Caution: If the temperature goes below 10 degrees for a few days, the apples may freeze.

Apple Tips

* Apples will not discolor if you place the slices in a pan of cold water with a pinch of salt for each whole apple used. Lemon juice sprinkled over the top of the slices will also stop discoloring.
* To remove discoloration from aluminum pans, boil apple peels in pan for 15 minutes.
* Boil apple slices in water to fill the house with a wonderful scent.
* If apples begin to shrivel, wash and place wet apples in plastic bag, close the bag, and refrigerate. They will be smooth and crisp again.
* If apples are not best eating quality, use them for pies, cobblers, and applesauce.

Apple Cooking Tips

* Layer thin slices of apple with potato slices for a tantalizing new taste for scalloped potatoes.
* Spread apple slices with peanut butter for a children's snack.
* Make an accompaniment for roast pork by grating raw apple and mixing it with lemon juice. Another delicious sauce is made by adding 1 part horse-radish to 4 parts applesauce.
* Puree equal parts grated apple and plain yogurt in the blender for a delicious treat.

(Thanks to Marlene Bennett, Alpine, Utah)

A-peel-ing Apple Basket

To dry apple slices: Choose good quality apples without blemishes for the most attractive apple slices. Jonathan, Golden Delicious, Red Delicious, Roman Beauty, or Gravenstein apples make the best apple slices. Slice apples either stem to bottom or around middle—slicing through the middle is attractive since the seed pattern is visible. Soak apple slices in mixture of 2 cups reconstituted lemon juice and 1 tablespoon salt to prevent apples from discoloring. Drain and dry. Dry on rack in oven at 140 degrees for 5–6 hours, leaving oven door ajar for ventilation. Slices should be leathery but not brittle.

To assemble basket: Choose a basket that has a fairly flat side surface in order to more securely adhere apple slices. Using a glue gun, glue apple slices around basket and over handle, overlapping the slices about 1 inch. Tie raffia around base of handles.

An Ancient Skill Revived:
Drying Foods for Preservation

There are a number of books on the market that give excellent directions for drying foods. Purchase a book or check at the library.

Hints for drying foods:

* To preserve color, dip pears, apples, or other white fruit in unsweetened pineapple juice before drying.
* Raisins can be made from the loose grapes at the grocery store that are sold at a lowered price. Ask the produce manager about buying these grapes. Seedless grapes should be used. Drying grapes in the sun is much faster than using a dryer.
* Fruit shrinks by two-thirds. Cut fruit in fourths.
* Put a mixture of flavored gelatin powder and sugar or sugar-cinnamon in a plastic bag with apples and shake until covered. Dry.
* Dry vegetables and mix together for a delicious soup mix. Dry each vegetable according to instructions. In order to determine how many dried vegetables to use, measure undried vegetables and then measure again after vegetables are dried. Keep track of proportion of shrinkage. Cook in water for reconstitution. Don't add salt until last half hour of cooking or vegetables will be too salty.
* To retain the color of potatoes, parboil 5–10 minutes before drying.
* To dry corn, pull back husks and hang in groups in basement. When you use corn, remove from husks using rubber gloves.
* Always dry vegetables when ripe but not overripe. If overripe, they will taste bitter. It is better for the vegetables to be slightly green than overripe.
* Fill a giant glass jar with dried fruits, coconut, and nuts—a nutritious snack for the family.
* Instead of raisins in muffins, use dried apricots or cherries.

Jan's Oven Drying Times

Apples	8 hours at 140 degrees
Apricots	10 hours at 140 degrees
Peaches	10–12 hours at 140 degrees
Pears	10 hours at 140 degrees

(Thanks to Jan Vincent, Alpine, Utah)

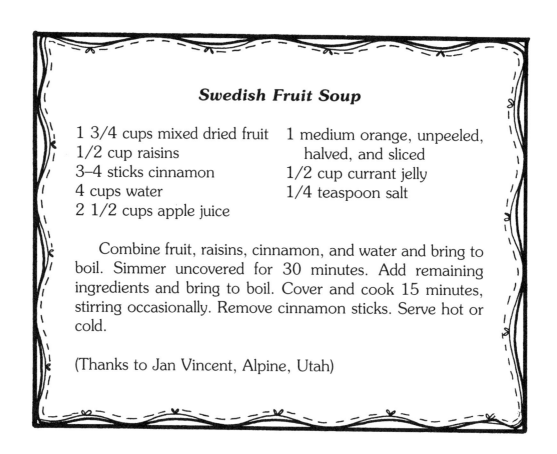

Swedish Fruit Soup

1 3/4 cups mixed dried fruit
1/2 cup raisins
3–4 sticks cinnamon
4 cups water
2 1/2 cups apple juice

1 medium orange, unpeeled, halved, and sliced
1/2 cup currant jelly
1/4 teaspoon salt

Combine fruit, raisins, cinnamon, and water and bring to boil. Simmer uncovered for 30 minutes. Add remaining ingredients and bring to boil. Cover and cook 15 minutes, stirring occasionally. Remove cinnamon sticks. Serve hot or cold.

(Thanks to Jan Vincent, Alpine, Utah)

Alternative Themes and Miniclasses

Theme: Little Red Schoolhouse

Invitation: Tie a ribbon and message around a piece of chalk. A cutout of a school-house could also be used as an invitation.

Miniclasses:

Brown-Bagging It. The start of school is an excellent time to teach a class on delicious and wholesome lunches.

Carry It! Make a flannel board carryall for family home evening.

Creative Book Bags. Make stencil canvas book bags for children.

Teacher Appreciation. Begin now to make Christmas gifts for children's teachers.

Theme: Have a Blue Ribbon Day . . . at Homemaking Meeting

Invitation: For an invitation, make a cutout of a badge and attach ribbons to it.

Miniclasses: The following miniclasses are planned as a round robin.

Scrumptious Scones. Scones with honey butter are delicious old-fashioned treats.

Back to Basics. Teach how to make homemade soaps. Check at the library for instructions.

Soap Foofaraw. Decorate your homemade soap or a purchased bar of soap with ribbon and flowers. Tie the ribbon around the soap and tuck flowers into the bow.

Quilting Bee. Teach how to put a quilt on the frames. A simple quilt block could also be demonstrated.

Cleaning Up. There are recipes for old-fashioned cleaning aids that work as well as the store-bought versions and are much more economical. You might check at the library or the local bookstore for a book on this subject.

October

Theme: Memories in the Making . . . at Homemaking Meeting

Invitation: A pattern for a house is included. Copy as necessary.

Miniclasses: October is National Family History Month, so have a round robin with miniclasses centered on family-oriented activities.

A Family Rooted in Tradition. Give tips on creating memories with meaningful family activities.

Where Do I Begin? Show how to get started on your children's memory books.

Who Am I? Writing your personal history is the topic of this miniclass.

Dear Diary . . . Share ideas to encourage personal journal writing.

From Trunk to Wall. Teach what to do with those family heirlooms.

A Family Rooted in Tradition

Two months before this meeting is scheduled, have the sisters submit their family traditions, which will be shared in a booklet. Type up the traditions and pass them out in the miniclass. From the submitted traditions, you should be able to find a sister who could effectively teach this miniclass. A book titled *Roots and Wings* by Helen Ream Bateman (Salt Lake City: Deseret Book Co., 1983; now out of print) might be available in one of the sister's libraries. It has excellent ideas for family traditions.

Family traditions. Many of the family activities recommended by the General Authorities naturally become fondly remembered traditions by children. Family prayer, scripture reading, family home evening, father's interviews and blessings, and countless other activities become treasured memories for family members.

Activities associated with holidays and seasons become traditions within a family. That special ornament that is *always* on the tree; the nativity that adorns the fireplace mantle; decorating cutout cookies at Christmas, which are then taken to favorite neighbors; a sleigh-riding outing in January; flying kites in March; making sugar panorama eggs at Easter; summer family reunions; an annual trip to view the beauty of the autumn leaves—all may become indelible memories that may eventually be traditions in a child's own home.

Secret love week. Family members draw names on family night. During the week they secretly do little acts of service for the person they have chosen. At the end of the week, they each guess who has their name.

Monthly date. Parents arrange their monthly schedule so that they have a "monthly date" with each child in the family. The undivided attention becomes a treasured memory for the children.

Family fitness. Let fitness become a traditional activity in the family. Regularly walk as a family. Tiny tots can be pushed in a stroller.

Mealtime memories. Be sure the family has dinner together every night, and make it a memorable occasion. Don't save centerpieces, candles, and fancy dishes only for company! At least once a week use your best china for the family's dinner. Don't just eat and run—spend time discussing the day's activities. In today's hectic environment, no activity could be more fondly remembered than a peaceful hour spent around the family dinner table. (See Elder LeGrand R. Curtis's talk "A Table Encircled with Love" in the May 1995 general conference issue of the *Ensign.*)

Service evenings. Spend one night a month as a family doing a service activity. It might be visiting an elderly shut-in in the area who does not have family near, helping an elderly neighbor with yard work, helping a single mother with yard work or repairs, taking dinner to an ill neighbor or helping him or her with the housework—there are innumerable opportunities for service all around us. Check with community service organizations and see if there are community projects that could be accomplished as a family. What an important family memory!

Where Do I Begin?

There are a number of excellent booklets and classes available on creating memory books. Check in your area at craft stores or at boutiques for information. There may be a sister in your ward who has done wonderful memory books for her children and would be willing to share her expertise.

Who Am I?

Have your ward genealogy expert teach a miniclass on writing your personal history.

Dear Diary

Encourage the sisters to begin writing in a journal. Have a sister who is diligent in this activity teach the miniclass.

From Trunk to Wall

Teach a class on various ways to preserve and display family heirlooms.

Alternative Themes and Miniclasses

Theme: It'll Haunt You . . . if You Miss Homemaking Meeting

Invitation: Draw a simple ghost outline and use as an invitation.

Miniclasses:

Spooky Treats from the Kitchen. Make Halloween holiday treats.

The Magic of Costumes. Demonstrate how to put together quick and easy costumes.

Halloween: It's in the Bag. Make trick or treat bags for children.

Halloween Craft Activity. Choose a holiday craft activity from the many available.

Theme: Come and Enjoy the Colors of Autumn . . . at Homemaking Meeting

Invitation: Use a simple leaf pattern for your invitation.

Miniclasses:

Autumn's Preserves. Jams and jellies make great Christmas gifts. Along with your recipes, show a variety of jar toppers for more festive giving.

Autumn's Glory. Create a door wreath made from dried fall foliage.

Autumn Makeovers. You can create a family wardrobe without straining the family budget. Make over seldom-worn items into children's clothing.

How to Stay out of the Red. Teach a class on budgeting and encourage the sisters to budget their Christmas spending.

November

Theme: Over the River and Through the Woods . . . to Homemaking Meeting We Go!

Invitation: A pattern is included for an old-fashioned sleigh. Copy and attach your message.

Miniclasses:

Turkey Tidbits. Teach how to prepare and serve that holiday bird, and what to do with all those leftovers!

Can-Do Candles. Make wintry candles out of recycled tin cans. These scented candles will fill your home with delightful yuletide smells.

Tabletop Extravaganza. Presentation is everything . . . learn how to make your table a work of art with table settings, napkin rings, centerpieces, place cards, and so on.

To Grandmother's House We Go. Make coming to grandmother's a treat! Learn how to be a super grandmother, and learn the balance between helping and interfering.

Turkey Pie

2 cups diced cooked turkey
1 can (4 1/2 ounces) sliced mushrooms, drained
1/2 cup sliced green onions
1/2 teaspoon salt
1 cup shredded natural Swiss cheese
1 1/2 cups milk
3/4 cups commercial all-purpose baking mix
3 eggs

Heat oven to 400 degrees. Grease a 10″ pie plate. Sprinkle turkey, mushrooms, onions, salt, and cheese in pie plate. Beat remaining ingredients until smooth, 15 seconds in blender on high or 1 minute with hand beater. Pour into plate. Bake until knife inserted between center and edge comes out clean (35–40 minutes). Cool 5 minutes. Makes 6–8 servings.

Turkey Surprise

4 tablespoons shortening
1/2 clove garlic, finely chopped
4 tablespoons flour
2 cups turkey broth
1 tablespoon soy sauce
3 cups diced cooked turkey

Melt shortening, add garlic and cook lightly. Stir in flour; cook until bubbly, stirring constantly. Add broth or chicken bouillon (1 bouillon cube in 1 cup boiling water). Cook until thickened, about 20 minutes. Add soy sauce and turkey. Serve over rice, waffles, fried noodles, English muffins, or biscuits.

Deviled Turkey

1/2 cup margarine
1/4 cup flour
1 teaspoon dry mustard
Dash nutmeg
2 cups milk
1/4 cup chopped parsley

3 tablespoons lemon juice
1 1/2 teaspoons salt
3 cups diced cooked turkey
1/2 cup bread crumbs
1 1/2 tablespoons margarine
1/2 teaspoon paprika

Melt 1/2 cup margarine; stir in flour, mustard, and nutmeg. Gradually add cold milk. Stir until thick. Remove from heat. Add parsley, lemon juice, salt, and turkey. Place mixture in a greased casserole. Combine crumbs and margarine and sprinkle over the turkey mixture. Top with paprika. Bake at 350 degrees for 15–20 minutes.

Can-Do Candles

Use small tin cans (8-ounce tomato sauce cans are a good size for votive candles). Wash the can in soapy, hot water and rinse well; rinse in a vinegar solution (1 part vinegar to 1 part water). Spray the can with 2 coats of primer, drying between coats. Spray with base color desired. Trace desired design onto tracing paper. Using graphite transfer paper, transfer pattern to can. Paint design with brushes or sponges, using acrylic paints. Use small paintbrushes for detail work. Allow to dry. Can also use three-dimensional decorations such as ribbon, string, candies, miniature greenery, buttons, and so on. Insert a scented votive candle and enjoy the delightful yuletide smells!

Alternate Themes and Miniclasses:

Theme: That Homemade Touch . . . Getting Started on Christmas!

Invitation: Cut two small mittens out of fabric that has been adhered to adhesive webbing. Attach the mittens, along with your message, together with string or ribbon.

Miniclasses:

Countdown to Christmas. Be ready to start the holiday season with an advent calendar. Numerous ones are available in stores, or be creative and make your own!

Festive Floor Cloths. Using artist's canvas primed on both sides (available at art supply stores), paint or sponge paint holiday designs to make a floor cloth. Secure edges to back side with E6000® adhesive sealant. When completed, apply 2 coats of spray varnish, drying between coats. Clean with a damp cloth as needed.

Wrap Yourself Up for the Holidays. Make holiday jackets out of sweat-shirts using one of the many available patterns.

Rise to the Occasion. Make yummy Christmas yeast breads to enjoy and to share with friends and neighbors.

Theme: Celebrate Autumn's Bounty . . . Come to a Harvest Festival!

Invitation: Attach your message to real nuts, Indian corn, small bags of candy corn, fruits, or similar items.

Miniclasses:

A Delicious Start. Get ready to start your holiday entertaining with a variety of hors d'oeuvre ideas.

Less Stress Through the Holiday . . . Mess. Teach how to organize your time for a less stressful holiday season.

Hassle-Free and Cost-Free Centerpieces. Show how to put together holiday centerpieces for your table using items you already have in your home.

Gratitude in a World of Plenty. Give family home evening ideas for helping teach children gratitude.

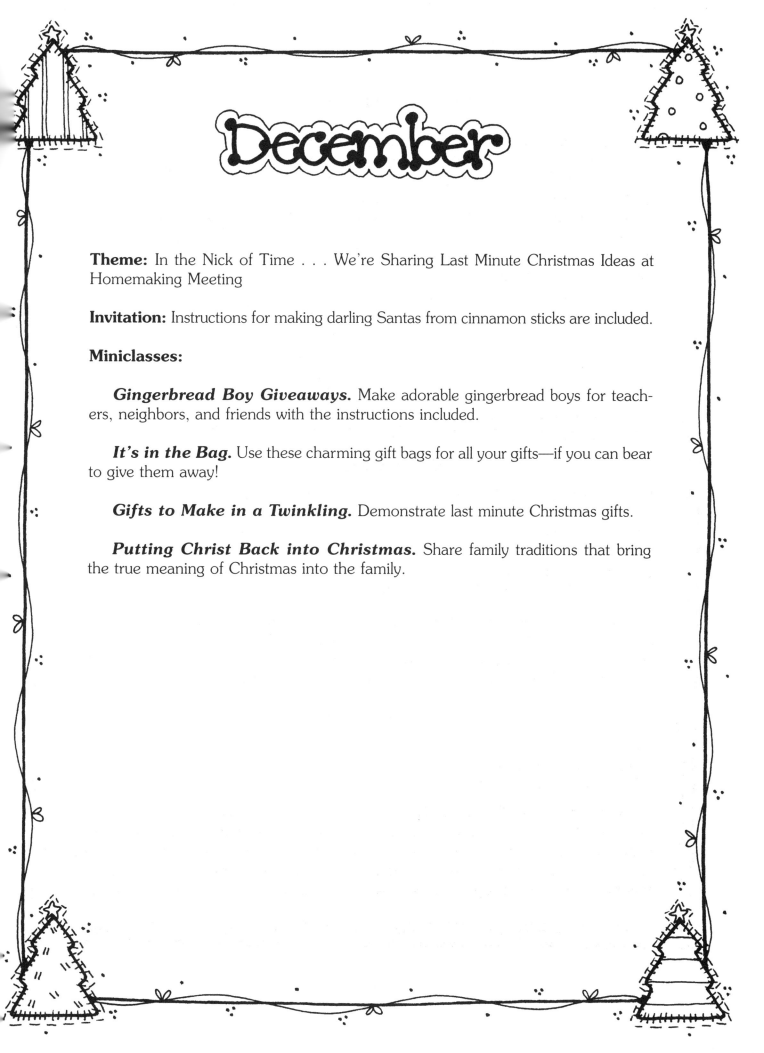

December

Theme: In the Nick of Time . . . We're Sharing Last Minute Christmas Ideas at Homemaking Meeting

Invitation: Instructions for making darling Santas from cinnamon sticks are included.

Miniclasses:

Gingerbread Boy Giveaways. Make adorable gingerbread boys for teachers, neighbors, and friends with the instructions included.

It's in the Bag. Use these charming gift bags for all your gifts—if you can bear to give them away!

Gifts to Make in a Twinkling. Demonstrate last minute Christmas gifts.

Putting Christ Back into Christmas. Share family traditions that bring the true meaning of Christmas into the family.

Cinnamon Stick Santas

Purchase cans of cinnamon sticks that are about 3″–4″ long (or cinnamon sticks of desired length). Using acrylic paints, paint entire stick red. If desired, you can leave the stick natural. Paint a small oval about 1/4 from top using flesh-toned paint. When this is dry, use a small paintbrush or stencil brush and stipple white paint around the face to add fur and a beard. Using the end of the paint brush or a toothpick, add small dots of black paint to make eyes. When completely dry, attach your message with raffia, adding a small bell.

Gingerbread Boys

1/2 cup butter, margarine, or shortening
1 cup brown sugar, firmly packed
2 teaspoons baking soda
2 teaspoons salt
1 teaspoon cinnamon
About 6 1/2 cups unsifted all-purpose flour

1 teaspoon ground ginger
1 teaspoon cloves
1 teaspoon allspice
1 1/2 cups (12 ounces) light molasses
2/3 cup water or apple cider

Using an electric mixer, cream together the butter, sugar, baking soda, salt, and spices until light and fluffy. Add molasses and beat until blended. Mix in the water or apple cider. Stir in flour, adding enough to make a fairly stiff dough. Chill several hours or overnight. (Makes about 3 dozen boys if using a 5″–6″ cookie cutter.)

Decorative Icing

1 egg white
2 cups powdered sugar
1/2 teaspoon cream of tartar

Beat egg white until very stiff. Gradually add the powdered sugar. Add the cream of tartar with the first of the sugar. Beat until frosting is smooth and holds peaks (about 5 minutes). This frosting hardens quickly and doesn't crush like buttercream icing. When using, keep the bowl of frosting covered with a damp cloth to keep it from hardening. If using pastry tubes, keep them also covered so frosting will not harden in the tube.

Gingerbread Boy Giveaways

When gingerbread dough has been chilled, roll out small amounts of dough at a time on a floured board or parchment paper to 1/8"–1/4" thickness. Using a purchased gingerbread boy cookie cutter (one with long arms and legs), cut out cookies. Transfer to a lightly greased baking sheet.

Cut plastic drinking straws into 1 1/2"–2" lengths. Insert a length of straw into each cookie near the top to make a hole for hanging. Do not remove the straw before baking.

Move and bend the legs and arms as desired to animate the boys. Add a length of straw under arms wrapped over the body to make room to insert a small candy cane under the arm. Again, do not remove the straw before baking. If desired, press raisins into the dough for buttons. Dip the raisins in slightly beaten egg white to make them stick better.

Bake at 350 degrees for 10 minutes or until lightly browned. Transfer cookies to wire racks to cool. Remove straws, making sure holes are entirely opened before the cookie cools.

When cookies have cooled, decorate as desired using decorative icing. Using a pastry tube, add buttons, hair, faces, names, and so on. Tie a ribbon through the hole at top for hanging. Add small candy canes in holes under arms.

These make cute old-fashioned Christmas tree decorations. They can also be put in plastic bags, tied with raffia or ribbon, and given as gifts to neighbors.

It's in the Bag—Gift Bags

Materials Needed:

HeatnBond® or Wonder-Under® adhesive webbing
Desired fabric
Purchased paper gift bags (ones with handles look great!)
Iron
Tissue paper (plain white)
Fine-line black marking pen
Glue gun and sticks or sticky glue
Acrylic paints
Buttons, charms, sequins, etc., for embellishing (small sticks make great snowman arms)

Trace patterns (those included, from clip art books, or patterns available for purchase) on paper side of adhesive webbing. Following the manufacturer's directions, fuse the fabric to the webbing. Cut out the designs and decide where you want them on the bag. If designs are layered over each other, start with bottom design. Remove the paper backing, place designs on the bag, cover with white tissue paper (to keep bag from scorching), and iron in place with a warm, dry iron. Glue on buttons, charms, and so on to embellish. Use acrylic paints and black marking pen to make stitching lines and do detail work. Tie with raffia or a torn fabric bow and add a fun, decorative tissue inside of the bag.

*Note: Use real sticks for arms.

Alternative Themes and Miniclasses

Theme: Come to Homemaking Meeting and Celebrate an Old-Fashioned Country Christmas

Invitation: Make a popcorn and cranberry wreath: String popcorn and cranberries on wire, making a wreath about 4″ in diameter. Tie a bow where wires connect, along with your message about homemaking meeting. Or glue the popcorn and cranberries to the edges of a construction paper circle. Glue a small bow on the wreath. Write your message in the center of the wreath.

Miniclasses:

Old-Fashioned Homemade Christmas Tree Ornaments. Make simple homemade ornaments for the tree with salt dough clay, cinnamon/applesauce clay, gingerbread, or decorated sugar cookies.

Old-Fashioned Homemade Gift Wraps. Make Christmas gift wrap using sponge painting or stamps.

Old-Fashioned Family Christmas Traditions. Share family Christmas traditions.

Popping Good Treats. Make popcorn treats from the kitchen.

Theme: A Sugarplum Christmas . . . at Homemaking Meeting

Invitation: Make gingerbread boy paper doll cutouts (with joining hands) out of brown paper bags. Write your message on the gingerbread boys (a message for each class on a separate boy), fold them up, and tie a ribbon around the neck. (The time and date should be on the first gingerbread boy.)

Miniclasses:

Snip and Snack Wreath. Teach a class on a variety of wreaths designed to hang in the entry of the home, so that when visitors leave your home during the holidays, they snip off a treat to take with them. Candy, cookies, purchased gingerbread boys—use your imagination!

Heavenly Morsels. Make homemade candies for the family or gift giving.

Festive Christmas Stockings. Be sure there is a stocking by the chimney for each member of the family. Have a demonstration showing a wide variety of stockings the sisters could make at home, or pick a simple pattern to make in class.

A Gift of Love. Present gift-giving ideas for the twelve days of Christmas.

Homemaking Department Survey

In order to better meet the needs of our Relief Society sisters, we are conducting a survey to find out what needs are not being met in our homemaking meetings. We would like to offer miniclasses that are meaningful and helpful, but without your input we cannot achieve this goal.

We urge you to spend thoughtful, prayerful time in filling out the survey. Think carefully about your strengths and weaknesses as a homemaker. Be honest. Try to assess the areas where you could use some help. You may not wish to put your name on your survey; if so, that is fine. Please return it as soon as possible.

HOMEMAKING

Strengthening Your Family Through Relief Society Homemaking

Name (optional) _____

Check your age category: 18–20 ___   21–30 ___   31–40 ___   41–50 ___
                          51–60 ___   61–70 ___   71–older ___

Do you work outside the home? ___   Full-time ___   Part-time ___

Do you prefer homemaking meeting at night? ___   Morning? ___

How would you feel comfortable participating in homemaking meeting?

  1. Just attend and socialize _____

  2. Teach a miniclass_____

  3. Subject you would feel comfortable teaching _____

  _____

  4. Would you be willing to assist someone else to teach a class? _____

  _____

Are you interested in genealogy miniclasses?_____

What is your level of expertise in genealogy?   Beginner ___   Advanced ___

Give suggestions for miniclasses that would interest you.

_____

_____

_____

_____

_____

_____

Is there someone with a special skill that you would like taught in a miniclass?

Name	*Skill/Talent*
_____	_____
_____	_____
_____	_____
_____	_____

The main purpose of this survey is to get input on what your goals as a homemaker are and what miniclasses will help you meet those goals. The following categories offer suggestions for miniclasses that may be interesting to you. Study the categories and check those classes that would most effectively meet your homemaking goals. Add any other classes you can think of in the blank spaces provided.

Cooking

( ) Serving balanced, nutritious meals
( ) Budget meals
( ) Quick to prepare meals
( ) Using coupons to cut costs
( ) Make ahead and freeze meals
( ) Emergency cooking
( ) Low-fat cooking

( ) Make-a-mix cookery
( ) Preserving food (drying)
( ) Preserving food (canning)
( ) Teaching children to cook
( ) Teaching missionaries to cook
( ) Diabetic cooking
( ) High altitude cooking

( ) Food storage use
( ) Wheat cookery
( ) Low-cost entertaining
( ) Fast, easy entertaining
( ) Family tradition cooking
( ) Microwave cooking
( ) Cake decorating
( ) Cooking with herbs
( ) Dutch oven cooking
( ) Gourmet cooking
( ) Yeast breads
( ) Quick breads
( ) Cookies
( ) Cakes
( ) Foreign foods
( ) Sourdough cooking
( ) Yogurt
( ) Fancy desserts
( ) Homemade ice cream
( ) Pastries

( ) Chicken
( ) Fish
( ) Vegetables
( ) Pasta
( ) Perfect pies
( ) Picnics
( ) Beverages
( ) Barbecue
( ) Hors d'oeuvres
( ) Soups
( ) Snacks
( ) Fruits
( ) Salads
( ) Candy
( ) _____
( ) _____
( ) _____
( ) _____
( ) _____
( ) _____

Managing Your Home

( ) Housecleaning tips
( ) Organizing your storage areas
( ) Getting your wash really clean
( ) Picture arranging
( ) Picture framing
( ) Houseplant care
( ) Furniture arranging
( ) Home decorating
( ) Organizing your housework
( ) Home finances—budgeting
( ) How to balance a checkbook and
bank statement
( ) Estate planning, wills, investments

( ) Simple home repairs
( ) Restoring furniture
( ) Flower arranging
( ) Energy saving tips
( ) Emergency supplies
( ) Filing
( ) Creating a history of your home
( ) Family traditions
( ) Teaching children to work
( ) Automotive maintenance
( ) _____
( ) _____
( ) _____

Sewing, Stitchery, and Quilting

( ) Basic sewing
( ) Finishing techniques
( ) Pattern making
( ) Learning about new sewing aids
available
( ) Beginning quilting
( ) Advanced quilting

( ) Crazy quilts
( ) How to put a quilt on a frame
( ) Holiday craft items
( ) Home decorating items
( ) Curtains
( ) Cross-stitch
( ) Shadow applique

( ) Knitting
( ) Tatting
( ) Bargello
( ) Trapunto
( ) Smocking
( ) Aprons
( ) Table linens
( ) Kitchen linens, hot pads, etc.
( ) Pillows
( ) Stuffed toys and dolls
( ) Teddy bears
( ) Doll clothes
( ) Soft sculpture
( ) Puppets
( ) Childrens toys

( ) Lamp shades
( ) Upholstery and slip covers
( ) Vests
( ) Sweatshirt jackets
( ) T-shirts
( ) Lingerie
( ) Decorating T-shirts
( ) Quilted wall hangings
( ) Braided rugs
( ) _____
( ) _____
( ) _____
( ) _____
( ) _____
( ) _____

Varied Interests

( ) Drying and using flowers
( ) Potpourri
( ) Pruning trees and bushes
( ) Perennials
( ) Wildflower gardens
( ) Roses
( ) Growing herbs
( ) Collecting and using seeds
( ) Forcing bulbs
( ) Planting and caring for bulbs
( ) Career development
( ) Resumes
( ) Balancing work and family
( ) Time management
( ) Photography
( ) Pursuit of excellence
( ) Preserving and displaying heirlooms
( ) Journal keeping
( ) Personal history
( ) Genealogy
( ) Family home evening helps
( ) Family scripture reading
( ) Learning to read music
( ) Learning to lead music
( ) Ceramics
( ) Basket making
( ) Tole painting
( ) Oil painting

( ) Watercolors
( ) Metal punch
( ) Stenciling
( ) Book reviews
( ) Grandmothering
( ) Volunteering in the community
( ) Adjusting to retirement
( ) Understanding menopause
( ) Friendshipping
( ) Language study
( ) Raising children alone
( ) Learning to live alone
( ) Caring for the elderly
( ) Personal appearance
( ) Exercise and diet
( ) Marriage enrichment
( ) Personal spiritual growth
( ) Scripture study
( ) Birthday parties and showers
( ) Children's literature
( ) CPR and first aid
( ) Decoupage
( ) Children's history books
( ) Restoring furniture and antiques
( ) Family reunions and newsletters
( ) _____
( ) _____
( ) _____

Homemaking Miniclass Schedule

Month						
Theme						
Luncheon Chairman						
Miniclass to coordinate with home management lesson						
Class #1						
Class #2						
Class #3						
Class #4						

Month _____ Date of Meeting _____

Theme _____

Responsibility	Person Assigned
Advertising (posters, etc.)	
Invitations or announcements (make and deliver to homemaking committee for delivery to homes)	
Miniclass sign-up sheets for Relief Society, Primary, and Young Women	
Announcements in Sunday ward bulletin and ward newspaper	
Display table for next month's miniclasses	
"Share Your Talent" or spotlighting display table	
Luncheon table decorations	
Thank you notes to miniclass teachers	

Miniclass Title _____ Teacher _____

A. Objective:
   1. State in a single idea what you want the sisters to understand and do.
   2. Discuss what you want them to learn, and challenge them to put the project into use. You might consider giving them an index card on which they can write down one idea or project to follow through with at home. Encourage them to tape the card where they can see it often until they have accomplished their goal.

B. Presentation:
   1. Show examples: Most people will get more excited about an idea or project if they see the completed item. Make displays as attractive as possible. Be enthusiastic about the things you teach, and your enthusiasm will be contagious. One of your responsibilities is to motivate the sisters to improve their skill levels.
   2. Show them how to do the project step-by-step, carefully covering each detail. Keep the project simple. Assume at this point that they have never done the thing you are teaching. Remember that what may seem easy to you can be confusing to an inexperienced sister.

C. Involvement: Have the class actually *do* something. Each student should be involved and have specific projects to work on. A teacher should try to find each sister's ability level and help her individually to reach her goals. When a technique is new, start with a simple learning project that can be learned quickly and give immediate satisfaction. Don't assume that a sister knows how to do something if she does not try it in class—diplomatically have each sister try the technique, first with your help and then alone until she feels comfortable with the technique. See that each sister who attends the class learns by doing.

D. Application: Encourage sisters to work at home between miniclasses on projects they select. Go the extra mile and help the sisters with their projects between homemaking meetings if necessary. You might provide each sister with a card on which you have written your telephone number and encourage her to feel free to call you if she has questions or needs help.

E. Helps and tools needed: Make a list of all the items you will need to take for your lesson. Check off the list as you collect the items so that you do not forget something. If you ask your class participants to bring their own materials for the involvement part of the lesson, make a complete list of what they will need, including instructions if needed, and get the list to them before homemaking meeting so that they have time to assemble or buy what is needed.

F. Handouts: Prepare a handout if applicable. Remember the curve of forgetting: the sisters will remember 50 percent the following day and 10 percent by the end of the week. Short, concise handouts will remind them of the steps involved in the project. The handouts should be easy to understand and not too long.

G. Additional resource materials: Make a list on your handout of books or other resource materials available and let the sisters know where they can find these materials: library, state extension service, etc. If special supplies are needed, list a variety of different places where they can obtain the supplies at reasonable prices. **Note: Remember that the Relief Society cannot promote a particular business or profit-making organization.**

Miniclass Title_____

Leader _____

A. Objective:
   1. _____
   2. _____

B. Presentation:
   1. _____

      _____

      _____

   2. _____

      _____

      _____

C. Involvement: _____

      _____

      _____

D. Application:_____

E. Helps and tools needed:

   _____   _____   _____

   _____   _____   _____

   _____   _____   _____

   _____   _____   _____

   _____   _____   _____

F. Handouts:_____

G. Additional resource materials:_____ _____

      _____